NOT YOUR
WHITE JESUS

NOT YOUR
WHITE JESUS

Following a Radical,
Refugee Messiah

SHERI FAYE ROSENDAHL

WJK WESTMINSTER
JOHN KNOX PRESS
LOUISVILLE • KENTUCKY

© 2018 Sheri DiGiacinto Rosendahl

First edition
Published by Westminster John Knox Press
Louisville, Kentucky

18 19 20 21 22 23 24 25 26 27—10 9 8 7 6 5 4 3 2 1

Book design by Drew Stevens
Cover design by Mark Abrams

Library of Congress Cataloging-in-Publication Data

Names: Rosendahl, Sheri DiGiacinto, author.
Title: Not your white Jesus : following a radical, refugee messiah / Sheri DiGiacinto Rosendahl.
Description: Louisville, Kentucky : Westminster John Knox Press, 2018. | Includes bibliographical references. |
Identifiers: LCCN 2018025270 (print) | LCCN 2018032064 (ebook) | ISBN 9781611648973 | ISBN 9780664264161 (pbk.)
Subjects: LCSH: Christianity—United States. | Jesus Christ—Person and offices.
Classification: LCC BR515 (ebook) | LCC BR515 .R575 2018 (print) | DDC 277.3/083—dc23
LC record available at https://lccn.loc.gov/2018025270

Most Westminster John Knox Press books are available at special quantity discounts when purchased in bulk by corporations, organizations, and special-interest groups. For more information, please e-mail SpecialSales@wjkbooks.com.

For Rich Rosendahl,

*thank you for showing me
what it can look like to love boldly.*

"Walk tall, kick ass, learn to speak Arabic,
love music, and never forget you come from a long line
of truth seekers, lovers, and warriors."
—HUNTER S. THOMPSON

CONTENTS

PART I

THE RADICAL,
REFUGEE MESSIAH

Chapter 1
NOT YOUR WHITE JESUS

Jesus is not a white guy. I hate to break it to you, but all those pictures you grew up seeing on the walls of your church or in your grandma's dining room showcasing the fair-skinned, blue-eyed, handsome, white Jesus are fabrications. They lied to you. Jesus isn't American; he's not even campaigning for America's greatness!

There's more. He actually doesn't care more about Americans than any other humans in the entire world (including Muslims and Communists). I'm serious—I checked the entire Bible and couldn't find one sentence pertaining to America being the most amazing nation ever in existence. I know, I was shocked too.

Blatant sarcasm aside, if you are like me, raised in a typical white American Christian home going to church every Sunday as a child, you know what I am talking about. If you didn't grow up in this fabricated, cookie-cutter context, but you grew up virtually anywhere in the United States, chances are you know what I'm talking about. If you grew up in a completely different culture and country but you have seen Americans on TV, chances are you *still* know what I'm talking about.

As a kid, I never differentiated Jesus from the Christianity I saw; to me they seemed one and the same. Christianity is a religion, and I've always felt some aversion toward religion. No matter how hard I tried, I never felt I belonged inside the walls of a church building. Though I was raised in an evangelical church, I felt like an observing outcast wondering why I heard talk of loving others but felt the weight of judgment and exclusivity. It wasn't all bad; I had some fun social times in youth groups, mostly meeting cute boys. I even believed the ABCs I grew up hearing in order to save my soul from eternal hellfire: A: Admit that you are a sinner in need of grace. B: Believe that God sent Jesus to die a bloody death for our sins. C: Confess Jesus as your Lord and Savior. When I was about four years old, I vividly remember sitting on an oversized maroon suede chair in my living room and essentially yelling at Jesus to get into my heart over and over again because I couldn't be sure if he was in there or not and I was terrified because— you know—the hellfire pit and gnashing of teeth and what not.

That was pretty much the extent of my involvement while growing up in the world of white Christianity. The American Church always felt like a place to be hurt, not a place for the hurting. From as far back as I can remember—a few real, spiritual moments in youth group aside—I always felt there was something more to this whole thing we call life, some sort of purpose that actually held meaning in this world. However, I definitely wasn't seeing that purpose—that radical, world-changing call—in church. I wasn't seeing Jesus. In the midst of Christianity, I somehow completely missed the ways of Jesus, and I don't think that I am unique in this.

The truth is, growing up in this supposed "Christian nation," it took me a quarter of a century to figure out who Jesus actually is. We tend to be a self-serving, money-driven, achievement-based, all-too-fearful nation, and there is a large section of the American Church that has followed right along, loud and proud, worshiping a made-up character I call White-Jesus.

To be perfectly clear, I'm not trying to debate Jesus' literal skin color. Jesus was born in Palestine, so it is safe to assume his skin was some shade of brown, but the White-Jesus ideology is much more than just mistakenly picturing Jesus as a Caucasian American. White-Jesus is the symbolic representation of a white-washed, Americanized Jesus that not all, but much of the American Church seems to follow. White-Jesus represents the conservative ideology that is controlled by white guys and dominates the American Church. It is an ideology that we see spread throughout the religion of Christianity, but it is also an ideology that is prevalent in our nation's politics.

White-Jesus Christianity stands firmly against health care for the vulnerable but is all about tax breaks for big business and spending millions and millions on its president's lavish "needs." White-Jesus Christianity is a crusader for the right to birth while blatantly disregarding a right to life as it writes off children slaughtered around the globe in American drone strikes as "collateral damage." White-Jesus Christianity strongly advocates for the deportation of immigrants who are simply trying to provide a life for their families, and it refuses refuge to the most vulnerable—giving them an essential death sentence—but increases in military funds are totally cool.

The White-Jesus ideology of American Christianity has largely failed when it comes to preaching and practicing the message of Jesus and collectively gets it wrong far more than right. Because of White-Jesus ideology, the term "American Christian" invokes thoughts of the vastly oppressive and even hateful philosophy that is imbedded not only in our culture, but in our political sphere, having an effect on the world as a whole. The severity of our situation should be blatantly obvious in the fact that American White-Jesus Christians have managed to bring to power a bigoted-misogynistic-racist sexual predator as the "leader" of this nation.

There are, for sure, many amazing Christians in the U.S. who are truly trying to follow Jesus to the depths of their soul. However, the version of Christianity dominating the U.S. religious landscape has failed to fulfill its basic self-proclaimed purpose. It has white-washed Jesus, dressing him in a $3,000 suit (made by workers earning pennies), with an American flag tie and boots made of alligator skin as he campaigns for capitalism and gun rights. That's often what we see in the major leaders of White-Jesus American churches, at least.

The thing is, it only takes a few minutes to flip through the pages of the Gospels to see how the person of Jesus has been distorted. The true message of this brown-skinned, Palestinian Jew is, in reality, the exact opposite of what is largely portrayed by the masses who follow White-Jesus American Christianity. The Jesus of the Gospels was actually a total badass in a countercultural, all-inclusive, anti-materialistic, radically loving kind of way. He was born to a teenage mother, fled as a refugee from an oppressive king, and amazed the most educated teachers when he was just a kid. People called him the Son of God, and yet he hung out with those that most people wouldn't even give a second look and was only really harsh on the self-righteous religious people.

When I finally discovered the Jesus of the Gospels and read his words, often printed in red letters, I found a love that changes everything, a love that can transform our world. Not in that awkward, "religiousy" way, but in a life-changing, joy-bringing, compassionate, humbling, almost poetic way. Jesus represents love—not Christianity.

Can you imagine what the world would look like if the thousands of Christian churches in this nation actually lived like Jesus? Generous with their funds, maybe housing the poor instead of spending millions of dollars on brand new fancy buildings? According to the National Center for Children in Poverty, around 21 percent of children in the U.S. live below the federal poverty line. That's close to 15 million children living below the poverty level—the second highest rate of child poverty of any developed nation.[1] That is appalling in itself, but in a nation that claims to follow the ways of a man who lived his entire life serving the poor, it is straight up shameful. What the actual hell, American Christianity? While mega churches produce multi-millionaire pastors, millions of children in their backyard can't afford to eat. Jesus never told anyone to take all their money and build bigger church buildings; he did, however, instruct people to give their money to the poor. How big of an impact would it make if we actually spent way less on buildings and gave way more to the poor?

The most important command Jesus specifically gave was to love your neighbor—this command was put on the same level as loving God—kind of a big deal. And what does loving your neighbor—the Great Commandment of Jesus—actually look like according to J-man himself? Jesus answered that exact question with the story of the Good Samaritan, so what if we looked at that story in the context of our world today? In modern-day terms, it would look something like finding a beat-up, half-dead ISIS leader on the side of the road, stopping, taking him in, bandaging his wounds, and spending your own money to have him cared for. Knowing he is your biggest enemy and showing him love anyway. That's a self-sacrificial kind of love.

* * *

Trying to live a life with Jesus means living completely counter to culture. It is both incredibly easy and incredibly difficult. It means that loving others takes priority over loving yourself in every way: your time, your hobbies, your money, your career. It means letting go of what the world's idea of what life should be, which can be a major struggle; at least it was for me.

For much of my life I worked my ass off to provide for my daughter (who I had very young—too young), do well in school, get my degree, and get a good job. My great goal was financial security, which in itself is not at all a bad thing. Through college, I was the girl who spent countless hours in coffee shops writing five-thousand-word practice essays contrasting U.S. foreign policy in the Middle East, Central America, and Africa until I had every essay option that I could possibly be given on my exams memorized so that regardless of the prompt I was given, I could fill out my body weight in blue books without missing a word. Yes, I had serious issues. Even worse, I actually enjoyed the tireless hours of studying, striving for perfection. Regardless, for a kid who literally did nothing through high school, the borderline crazy hard work paid off, and I graduated with a BA in history with high honors. I also minored in education, because what else are you going to do with a bachelor's degree in history?

However, after all that hard work, I had trouble becoming state certified to teach because I couldn't afford to forego paid employment while fulfilling the student teaching requirement. Despite my lack of full certification, thanks to a former professor, I got referred to some high schools for interviews. My goal had been financial security for my family and I needed a good stable job, but there were going to be some major walls I had to get through. There were the obvious facts that I was not fully certified and that there is not exactly a shortage of history teachers desperately searching for jobs. On top of it all, I got insanely nervous in every interview. It was awkward. After a few months of interviewing and summer coming to an end, I got a call from an urban alternative high school that worked strictly with at-risk students.

I was definitely considered at-risk in my own high school years, and this happened to be the demographic I wanted to teach more than any other. This was essentially my dream job in the world of education, so I got past my inherent nervousness and, when asked why they should hire me, I got some serious swagger and bluntly said, "You very well may find someone with more teaching experience than I have, however, you will not find anyone who has as much passion, commitment, and belief in these kids as I do." It was a small mic drop moment that apparently worked, because they hired me. The university I went to even ended up working with me so that I could become state certified under some unique terms.

I had the most amazing students and loved being their teacher. I excelled in the profession, and my kids' success rate basically doubled from that of the year before. Despite the odds being against me, I achieved what the world would call success, and on top of that I finally had that stable financial security I deeply desired.

Over time, however, the pressure of the state's obsession with standardized test scores became increasingly draining. I found meaning in my job through the relationships with my students, not in trying to cram a bunch of information into their heads that could be passionlessly regurgitated in the form of mindlessly bubbling in seventy-something multiple choice answers. In the depths of my soul, I knew it was time for a change. Do you ever feel like that? Like there is more to this thing we call life?

It was time to get back in touch with a passion I'd set on the back burner during my years teaching.

I had always had a flame for social justice. One night, as a somewhat ignorant young college student, while trying to work out, I watched some random documentary on Iraq and that flame exploded into a massive ball of fire as if someone had thrown a bottle of kerosene onto it. My heart broke for Iraq and its people, and I needed to learn more. I wanted a better understanding. So I began taking as many classes as I possibly could on the Middle East and the lovely Arabic language (which, after four years of classes and the ability to read and write, I still can't speak). As I progressively learned more about the Middle East, I made some amazing friends and fell in love with the people and the culture. After a trip to Palestine toward the end of college, my heart's greatest desire became clear: I really wanted to be part of the change our world needs. I wanted to do anything in my power to extend love to the amazing people who were displaced from their homes in the Middle East. I wanted to be involved with refugee work. My greatest passion became and continues to be pursuing peace and embracing the way of genuine love with our neighbors from the Middle East who have become refugees, often because of circumstances involving our own nation. The people I have encountered through this passion are some of the most amazing, kind, strong people in this world, and it's inexcusable that much of our society has turned their backs on or labeled them "the other."

Though this became my greatest passion, I didn't really know where to start or how I could support my daughter doing that kind of work, so this desire sat on the sideline as I finished college and started my teaching career.

A few years went by before I noticed a friend of a friend on Facebook who ran a nonprofit working with refugees. I reached out to him, curious about his work, and after we realized we had a ton in common, especially our shared love of the Middle East, one thing turned into another and we began dating. The thing was, Rich lived in Iowa and I lived in Texas, so after a year and a ton of airfare, we decided to get married and that I would move up to the great state of Iowa at the end of the school year. At that point, I was faced with a choice: I could find a new teaching job in the Midwest, even though I felt my passion and purpose already fading, or I could do something different. I could let go of a good career that offered me financial security and seek something more, working alongside my amazing husband. However, the choice wasn't that cut and dry: nonprofit work doesn't tend to pay a ton, and Rich's income was marginal. If I decided to join Rich, the financial stability I had worked so hard for would be gone, by choice. It took some time to find the courage, but ultimately, I said, "F-it" and gave up that job that provided me financial security in order to work part-time subbing (glorified babysitting) so I could pursue something I deeply believed I was supposed to be doing—humanitarian work with refugees from the Middle East.

I took quite a bit of criticism over my decision—many times from Christian types—and I understand that in our culture of achievement, this change in my life looked dumb. But honestly, I didn't care too much. No one has ever done anything truly meaningful without taking big risks. If you look at the teachings and life of Jesus, giving up financial security to follow his ways and love others is pretty on point. Peter, Andrew, James, John, and Matthew literally walked off their job sites to follow Jesus. You don't think that was a risk to their financial security? So, regardless of any risks, stress, and being thought of as an idiot, making the decision to pursue something I deeply believe in has brought immense joy to me and my family.

Since taking that step of faith, I have continued to discover a better understanding of who the real Jesus is. You don't have to look far (basically read any of the Gospels) to realize that the Middle Eastern Jewish man who lived two thousand years ago and went by the name of Jesus lived a radically minimalist life of bold, risky love. And to follow this guy on whom a major religion is based is to live a life boldly loving others first, regardless of how countercultural it might look in our White-Jesus society. This narrow road is hard and crazy, but the value and purpose to be found is indeed the pearl of great price. It's worth it completely.

* * *

Though I grew up in the American Church, I never really fell into religion; I think I sensed the hypocrisy from a pretty young age. My husband, Rich, on the other hand, has a very different story. He grew up in the middle-of-nowhere Iowa, a super handsome, charismatic athlete (in the '90s when jocks were apparently a big deal) and pretty much partied through high school and college. He then spent most of his twenties chasing the benjamins and was incredibly successful building that consumerist idea of the American life that we are told we are supposed to want.

In his late twenties, Rich's world fell apart overnight. He was married with two young kids and had all the material and career success in the world. The problem was he never really was able to deal with the anxiety of the world without booze, and he drank constantly. Eventually, his wife understandably was sick of it, and she left him. He should have seen it coming, but addiction can blind you from reality, so he was caught completely off guard. He was a mess after losing his family, and one night he had a unique, Paul-like encounter in his basement. He began to follow Jesus and quit drinking literally overnight (which is insane considering the amount he drank). He then left his high-paying job in medical sales in order to become a better father for his kids.

After Rich randomly started following Jesus, not really knowing where to start, a former coworker of his heard what was going on and told him to check out a certain church because "the pastor used to be a really good wrestler." Wrestling is really big in Iowa. So Rich stumbled into an evangelical fundamentalist movement and quickly fell into hardcore religion. He became a Neo-Calvinist, was really into the masculine Christianity movement, thrived in the use of apologetics, and began taking master's level seminary courses. He was basically a poster boy for White-Jesus American Christianity.

Luckily, it didn't last. There came a point when Rich realized that what he saw in the American White-Jesus Church and what he saw in the red letters didn't align, and one day all the theology he thought was "the way" came crashing down. Rich was attending a talk by Carl Medearis, an expert on Arab-American and Muslim-Christian relations who has spent years in the Middle East and has written some great books. This was around the time of the Libyan uprising, and Rich was super interested. After the event, Rich went up to Carl and said, "So you are going to Libya?" Carl looked him dead in the eyes and said, "Yeah, why don't you come with me?"

It was one of those life-changing moments when something as simple as an invitation makes you realize you can do more than you ever imagined. Rich was in. He and Carl exchanged information, and he planned on going to the Middle East for the first time.

In a United Nations refugee camp in the middle of the Tunisian desert along the Libyan border, he had a conversation with a stoic, statuesque man that would change the course of Rich's life forever. It started with a general question that everyone was asked: Had the man come to the camp alone, or was his family with him? In a straightforward manner the man informed them his family was no longer with him. He further went to explain the brutality, suffering, and execution of his family that he had witnessed firsthand. Though his life may have been spared, his punishment was worse than death. As my husband looked into the eyes of this man, he was silenced, unable to say a word. There was hollow hopelessness in the man's almost lifeless eyes that he had never encountered. What words could be said? Though Christianity had "trained" him for circumstances such as this, there was no adequate response for what he had just heard.

This conversation haunted Rich as he came to realize that the commitment to understanding Christian theology had become a blatant distraction to the true purpose of following Jesus: love. Simply loving others. All his training had not helped him become more loving to those like this man; rather, it was an attempt at a modern day manifest destiny, basically conquering people who are *not like us* with the intention of making them *more like us*. Though his desire was always to love, his theology and deep religious roots subtly but completely contradicted the Great Command of Jesus. Realizing this disconnect, Rich detoxed and found his way into a life of truly trying to follow the red-letter Jesus.

I didn't meet my husband until after this transition; he is the kindest, most genuine, loving man I have ever encountered. Honestly, it's hard for me to imagine him as a raging conservative Christian. If we would have met earlier in life, someone definitely would have had a drink thrown in his face.

Through Rich's transition, he ended up starting a nonprofit called The Nations, which is dedicated to peace and humanitarian work, both domestically and abroad, with refugees from the Middle East and North Africa. His work has taken him all over the world in a quest to love, serve, and learn from our amazing neighbors who have been displaced from their nations for various tragic reasons. You can probably see now why we fell for each other. That, and he is the most amazing cook in existence.

Like Rich and me, there are many out there with completely different backgrounds who have somehow come to the understanding that the ways of the red-letter Jesus are dramatically different from those of the American Christian White-Jesus. With the mess that is our world, it is more than time for us to re-examine the ways of Jesus in contrast to what we see in the ideology of our self-proclaimed, so-called Christian nation.

* * *

This book is an invitation to look again at the Gospels' red letters—without all the religious crap. Focus on the ways of Jesus and question what you have been told you are supposed to believe in light of what you see through the teachings of the radical refugee Messiah. You very well may not (let's be real, you will probably not) agree with everything that I say, and that is awesome. I don't know everything. In the grand scheme of the universe I probably know close to nothing. What I do know is our world is a mess, and White American Christianity is a mess. I could be wrong, and if someone could explain how these self-proclaimed American Christian views of White-Jesus align with the true Jesus, please enlighten me. But to be real, if you wondered why it took me twenty-five years to figure out Jesus when I was surrounded by Christianity, there is your explanation—American Christianity is not synonymous with the ways of the Jesus we see in the red letters.

Though my stance on many topics will be apparent, my purpose is not to convince you that I am right but to provoke thought, conversation, and hopefully a revolution in regard to the hurt we are seeing in our world because of the White-Jesus fabrication.

This is why I am writing this book. I want us to look at some of the issues that are being proclaimed by the ideology of White-Jesus American Christianity and examine how this ideology relates to the ways of the true Jesus. Salvation, self-protection, humility, judgment, consumerism, race, war, sexuality, abortion, immigration—all topics the general American Church has a vocal and clear way of approaching. But what do the red letters say? Where is Jesus and where is White-Jesus?

This book is divided into to two sections: The first deals with what Jesus said was our greatest command and how we can go about truly being the change we need in this world in better alignment with the red letters. The second deals with some of the above-mentioned important questions on various issues in our society that we need to consider rethinking from a red-letter perspective. Throughout the chapters of this book, there are questions to help you reflect and process, as well as a discussion guide at the back of the book. You can read this book solo, with a friend or group of friends and process together. Your thoughts, interpretations, and views matter!

It is largely because of the ideology of White-Jesus Christianity that this nation is more divided than ever. Instead of seeing love, we are drowning in hate. White-Jesus Christianity has created a climate that contradicts the red letters; it's incredibly exclusive and full of condemnation and hypocrisy. It's time to go against the grain and be the change you want to see.

You were made for more than a life of mediocrity. It's time to go back to the basics, drop the weird religious crap, and focus on the red letters. This is where we will see true, meaningful change in our world, a revolution based on bold, red-letter love. So let's explore Jesus, the real red-letter Jesus, not your white Jesus.

Chapter 2

MEET THE BROWN-SKINNED, PALESTINIAN, RED-LETTER JESUS

Let's talk a bit about the Jesus of the red letters who was born a little over two thousand years ago in a little town called Bethlehem. We all know Jesus was Jewish, but what many people don't know is that Jesus was also Palestinian. You see, Bethlehem is in Palestine, both today and when Jesus was born. Jesus was born under Roman occupation in the land that the Romans referred to as Palestine. All of the inhabitants of the region, both Jewish and non-Jewish, were Palestinian because that's where they were from—Palestine.

Maybe part of why many white, American Christians think of Jesus as white is that many modern Jews in Israel are of European descent, but the Jesus of the red letters probably would look a lot like someone from Iraq or Jordan does today. In fact, if Jesus tried to travel from his homeland to the U.S. today, a young, poor, single, brown refugee man from the Middle East, I doubt we would let him in. In fact, we currently have a ban on people who look just like him.

Now, if Jesus was a blond-haired, blue-eyed Israeli man, we would welcome him no problem. But he wasn't. What we know today as Israel didn't come into existence until 1948. After World War II, the UN decided that the Jewish people understandably needed a homeland. The problem was that to make a nation-state for the Jewish people, land that Palestinians of all faiths had called home for hundreds of years was taken away. The kingdom of ancient Israel that the Israelites called home fell hundreds of years before Jesus was even born and thousands of years before modern Israel or Israelis even existed.

Because of the land taken and Palestinians being exiled from their homes, the creation of modern Israel initiated a conflict known as the Israeli-Palestinian conflict that has lasted for over a half of a century. Today, Palestine consists of three areas: the Gaza Strip that Israel has isolated from resources and basically the world; the West Bank, which is Palestinian controlled but from which Israel continues to illegally take land while building illegal settlements and a massive wall (also deemed illegal by the international community); and then there is East Jerusalem, which is largely Palestinian but under the control of Israel.

As I dove into my studies of the Middle East in college and began to learn the history of the Israeli-Palestinian conflict, it made sense that—given my slant toward social justice—this issue became one that I was incredibly passionate about.

For decades Palestinians have been treated as less than human by the modern nation of Israel. Palestinian children are arrested and imprisoned by the Israeli government for years without reason; drones bomb Gaza regularly and Gaza flings random missiles toward Israel; and the Israeli army regularly invades the West Bank, raiding homes, shooting rubber bullets (sometimes live bullets), and gas into the streets of civilian neighborhoods. It's an apartheid state, one which is basically funded and strongly supported by the American White-Jesus Church with its weird Christian Zionist ideals.

You know, I can vividly remember my reaction the first time someone, a person who is dear to me, tried to convince me that the Jewish people need to rule the land of Palestine, establishing a nation-state, in order for Jesus to come back. As I stood in a dimly lit hallway listening intently, my stomach dropped. I thought, *is this real life?* I felt instantly, simultaneously confused and appalled. Basically, "we" need to help Israel conquer Palestine and Palestinians at any cost or God is not going to send Jesus back and bring the "end times." With this type of thinking, people of Jewish descent are favored by God, and we need to support the modern nation of Israel regardless of their inhumane treatment of others.

So, after this Christian ideology was explained to me for the first time, with no hesitation and I'm sure no chill, I responded with a couple of blunt but serious questions: "Are you telling me that God cares for one group of people more than others based on their blood line? Well how pure does one's blood have to be at this point to be part of this group of chosen ones? Wow, so what you're telling me is that God is prejudiced based on factors completely out of our control?"

By the end of the conversation, after my fiery disposition had wound down, I had come to a new conclusion, which I calmly expressed, "If the Christian God is essentially racist, then I have no interest in *your* God." It wasn't a declaration of atheism as much as a declaration against the idea that God could be a bigot; why would anyone want to follow that God? Though I had grown up in the evangelical church, I was still lacking in my understanding of the ways of Jesus; for all I knew, he was also a raging bigot. I mean, so many of his so-called followers clearly were.

It was 2012 before I truly came to understand that Jesus was not like his followers. At the time I probably would have been considered a pretty loud and fiery liberal. I loved the Middle East, the people, the culture, the shisha, the tea. After all that I had seen from "Christians," I had the firm idea that anyone who called themselves a Christian was a dispensationalist Zionist who probably hated Muslims and whose sole purpose in having a conversation with anyone from "that part of the world" would be to try to convert them manifest-destiny style. Yeah, pretty intense.

When I was twenty-five, my mom married the only pastor I had ever truly respected. I truly respected him because I knew he genuinely loved people, which (unfortunately) seemed really unique in that world of pews and crosses. At their wedding I was introduced to a man who runs a well-known Christian organization doing peace work with Muslims, and I was invited to a conference the following weekend. Oddly, I felt like I had to go. I was more than a little skeptical of these Christians trying to love Muslims. I had seen enough White-Jesus Christian propaganda about trying to sneakily convert others, and I wasn't about to buy into it so easily. With this mentality, I arrived at the conference with walls in high gear, ready to unleash my fiery, passionate (unwavering, sarcastic, argumentative) side toward anyone who began talking about trying to convert Muslims, or convert anyone, for that matter.

To my great surprise, what I found was something unexpected. What I found changed something inside of me; it was the first glimpse I had of what it could mean to truly follow the ways of Jesus, the refugee Messiah.

What I found was a group of people who hung out in mosques, not to convert, but to literally love their neighbors as Jesus would, without judgment, without a deeper agenda, and without weird American fear based on false propaganda that demonizes Islam. Just people hanging out with people without letting labels get in the way. I found real people who said they were Christians but also opposed the oppression of Palestinians.

Wait, so all Christians aren't Zionists?

It was the start of my paradigm shift. Jesus loves the Middle East, which makes sense because that's his homeland, and Jesus loves Muslims because Jesus loves everybody, and there are people who actually get that and live their lives trying to follow this Jesus. In other words, I found that there were people who claimed Christianity and were actually normal-ish, kind humans and not weirdos with a manipulative messiah complex.

My new revelation of who real-life Jesus was didn't end there. I ended up joining some of these red-letter-Jesus-following types of Christians on a trip to Palestine, where I learned and saw firsthand the vast, disgusting, dehumanizing state of occupation in the region. The West Bank is basically an open-air prison, but despite their circumstances, the Palestinians I met held a spirit of unimaginable hospitality and love; they were the most generous and kind people on this planet. My heart was incredibly heavy the entire trip, as it should have been.

It was in this place where my paradigm shift came full circle. I was standing on the shore of the Sea of Galilee, the place where Jesus used to chill with his buddies, watching the water rise and fall over my feet, when something inside of me finally clicked. I had an intense, almost unexplainable flow of peace overwhelm me as I realized more deeply that the American Church of White-Jesus, the one that I saw hurting people, judging people, justifying oppression at every turn, was in no way like the actual Jesus. The real, brown-skinned, Palestinian refugee guy who lived 2000 years ago was different. This guy was love. Not just any love—bold love. And I actually wanted to follow him.

* * *

When I came home, my journey in trying to learn the ways of the Jesus of the red letters continued; I couldn't get enough of this guy, and the more I learned of him, the less a lot of American Christianity made sense.

You see, in the world of Christianity I had never even known (or even really saw) the Great Commandment of Jesus, which is tragic in itself. Jesus was pretty clear about what the greatest commandment is:

> "You shall love the Lord your God with all your heart, and with all your soul, and with all your mind." This is the greatest and first commandment. And a second is like it: "You shall love your neighbor as yourself." On these two commandments hang all the law and the prophets.
>
> Matt. 22:37–40

On these *two* commandments hang all the laws, y'all. All of them.

This whole time the Great Commandment of Jesus— the guy who the American Church claims to follow—has been to love others. He put it on par with loving God—kind of a big deal. So how did so much of the ideology of the White American Church seem to miss this entirely? Why do so many focus on a fabricated White-Jesus who is out to convert, condemn, and apparently obsess over who people have consensual sex with or what bathroom they use?

This is not the Jesus we see in the Bible. The Jesus of the red letters said, "I give you a new commandment, that *you love one another*. Just as I have loved you, you also should *love one another*. By this everyone will know that you are my disciples, if you have *love for one another*" (John 13:34–35, italics added). I don't know how much more clear Jesus could have been about love here. Seriously, I know it sounds like some stoner hippie stuff, but Jesus wasn't messing around, it really is all about loving one another.

I could be wrong. To be fair, the American White-Jesus Church has seminary-trained, super-religious, Christian experts interpreting this stuff, and I'm just some random person. Really, what do I know? I guess trying to figure out Jesus should be super difficult and only for the highly educated theologians, you know, like his original followers were . . .

Oh wait, Jesus' crew consisted of fishermen, zealots, tax collectors, prostitutes, and basically anyone off the street. I wonder where they went to seminary.

My point in this clear sarcasm is to say that we don't need some elitist religious type to tell us how we should understand Jesus. The red letters are for anyone and everyone. The religious elitist types of Jesus' day didn't get it, but the completely regular people that Jesus taught did. They heard him say to love one another, love as he loved them. Jesus ate, hung out with, and even healed the normal folk, many of whom the religious elite wouldn't even look at. He set the bar pretty damn high when he spent his time outside randomly teaching about love for days straight, bringing dead people back to life, and feeding the hungry. To follow Jesus' ways of love, we will always be growing in our attempts to love boldly.

So how would we say Jesus loved? Well, the generic White-Jesus Christian answer would be something like, "He loved us so much that he died on the cross to forgive our sins so that we don't burn in Hell for flipping ever" or something along those lines. Christianese aside, sacrificing your life to love others is probably some of the boldest of love. Regardless, I don't think we need to go out searching for a rescue scene that ends with saving a baby from a burning building with our own demise in the process. There is so much more to the ways of Jesus than his willingness to face an incredibly brutal death.

Basically, the way of Jesus is a self-sacrificial kind of love. It means we put loving others above loving ourselves. We love without return, with zero expectations or motive of any type of gain.

Let me tell you a story. This one time, Jesus was hanging out watching people drop cash into what would be the equivalent to a church offering basket—a temple tithing box. Basically, he was people watching at the temple and a bunch of loaded people came by, throwing in benjamins. As he was watching, a poor widow also came by and threw in a few cents. Jesus, being a badass, called his disciples over and said,

> "Truly I tell you, this poor widow has put in more than all those who are contributing to the treasury. For all of them have contributed out of their abundance; but she out of her poverty has put in everything she had, all she had to live on."
>
> Mark 12:41–44

When I think of sacrificial love, I often think of this story. My husband and I run a nonprofit that works with refugees, as I have mentioned, and our organization is fully supported by everyday, amazing individuals. Some of our partners are incredibly well off financially and give generously; they are amazing, and we appreciate them incredibly. But do you know who I appreciate even more? Our partners who literally have almost nothing, yet they still support our work financially because they deeply believe in loving others first. They are the most amazing people, who joyfully give everything to love others. They are the kingdom.

Sacrificial love is about radical generosity, and it always changes the world.

Think about some of the things Jesus said: give to anyone who asks, turn the other cheek, walk another mile, if they want your shirt give them your coat as well (Matt. 5:38–42). All of these things require this sort of disposition of sacrificial generosity, and, don't be fooled, this is hard for us. If we are being honest, we generally tend to kind of suck at it.

Imagine all the times when you have been at a stoplight and seen a man with a cardboard sign asking for money, standing in the burning heat, and you can tell from the deep lines on his face that life hasn't been easy on him. What do you do? Some may feel pity, some may give him one of those emergency homeless people bags that churches give out with tuna and a toothbrush, but how many would give him money? I mean, he asked for money. "But what if he uses it for drugs?" you say. "What if he goes and buys booze and meth? We can't enable that, can we?" Well, that is a thousand percent your decision. But from where I stand, I didn't see Jesus make an exception to the "give to anyone who asks" guideline. He didn't say give to anyone who asks as long as you know that whatever they are going to do with that money is something you would personally approve of. It's not give with stipulations; it's give generously and then give more.

Man, that's a difficult mentality for most of us Westerners. It's like we always have this anxiety about making sure we're taken care of first and then whatever we have left over, not including the stuff we need to save "just in case," we can be generous with. We tend to only be generous if we first make sure our needs are covered, and then our possible future needs, and any of our wants, and any of our possible future wants. We would like to have that sort of feeling of security for ourselves first, then we can give to others.

I would love to say that I have never had any issues putting others above my own sense of security, but that would be a point-blank lie. This is definitely something I personally have struggled with in my life.

As a single, teenage mom just starting out, I felt I had to work hard, save, basically be stingy and make sure we were constantly better-than-good financially or the world would fall apart. So when I read Jesus' words about not storing our treasures on earth but in heaven and that where our treasure is our heart will also be (Matt. 6:19–21), I was like, *damn.* Though I was by no means wealthy, my treasure was in financial security and the more security I had, the more I felt I needed, and that's where my heart was too. This realization felt gross.

Slowly I began to give up this nature of control and take risks to grow and learn how to love generously first. I had to trust that our family would be fine even if I didn't obsess over finances and that loving others—giving to anyone who asked, anyone with a cardboard sign or otherwise, more purposefully seeking out situations where I could be generous, learning to give and give more, and increasingly going outside my comfort zone—took priority over my excessive control of money. Honestly, when I met my husband, he taught me a lot about how radical generosity could look. It was not an instantaneous transformation of the heart for me. It started with the simple, yet uncomfortable, realization of where my heart truly was, and gradually I learned (and am still learning) to take more and more risks to become more intentionally bold in loving others generously, even when it feels counterintuitive or even kind of irresponsible. The reality is that it is never wrong to give something up in order to love someone else; you can't be too generous with love.

Self-sacrifice—particularly when it comes to our finances—is completely countercultural to our mentality of shallow egocentrism that tells us we constantly need more. Maybe that's why Jesus said it is easier for a camel to fit through the eye of a needle than for someone who is rich to enter the kingdom of God (Matt. 19:23–24). Maybe that's why he told some people to sell their crap and give it to the poor. He knew how hard it would be, but he also knew how liberating it would be if we stopped clinging to our material wealth and embraced a life completely contradictory to what society tells us.

* * *

I often think of Jesus' first disciples and what it looked like for them to decide to follow him. So there is Jesus, taking a stroll on the beach, and he sees two brothers fishing, not like for sport; they were fishing because that was their job. So Jesus says something like, "Hey y'all (obviously he didn't actually say y'all, he was not a Texan, but he probably said the Aramaic equivalent to y'all, because it's a great word), follow me, and I will make you fishers of men." Fishers of men? What the hell does that mean? Like cannibalism? Well, apparently Simon and Andrew were intrigued, because they left their job site immediately and followed him. Crazy, right? It didn't stop there; Jesus walked farther down the beach and saw James and his brother John sitting in their boat mending their nets with their dad, Zebedee, and some hired help. So he called them, and they essentially ditched their father, leaving him with the hired help, and went follow Jesus.

Now that's the version of Mark and Matthew; in Luke's version of events Jesus jumped in one of their boats while teaching and then basically shocked everyone when he told Simon, who had been fishing all night and caught not a damn thing, to cast his net in the deep and then their nets overflowed with fish. It was then that all the guys ditched their boats, leaving everything to follow Jesus. So, with a miracle type event in play, it makes a little more sense why they left everything at their job site to follow Jesus, but nonetheless, they left their means of livelihood to follow this rando. They essentially sacrificed life as they knew it to follow Jesus, learn from him, and love others.

Can you imagine being at work, sitting at your computer or whatever you work on, staring at Facebook on your phone, when some dude walks by and solves some intense problem you have been working on for days, and then asks if you want to follow him. Would you literally leave your job? Probably not. The thing is, most of us have a hard time sacrificing any of our personal time to boldly follow Jesus, let alone being radically generous sacrificing all of the busy-ness of our world to follow his ways first.

Look, I am not going to tell you that learning to personally make sacrifices to follow the way of red-letter love is going to be easy, and I am not telling you to quit your job or to sell all your crap. I am, however, going to tell you to consider how it could look to love a little bolder. What could you sacrifice to love others generously over yourself?

I hate to use this comparison because I know how amazingly lame it is, but I think "YOLO" applies here. You only live once. Real talk, we only have this one life, and if we want to follow the ways of the true Jesus, then we might as well go all in and take his Great Command seriously. It's that radically generous sacrificial love that brings life; it's that "pearl of great price" that Jesus talks about. If you have encountered radically generous love, you know that no matter how grand or small it may look, it changes something in your soul.

My husband and I take teams to the Syrian border to love, serve, and learn from our Syrian neighbors who are refugees. The people we meet are absolutely amazing, and radical generosity is embedded into their culture in the most beautiful way. We hang out with a ton of beautiful families who truly embody what it looks like to love others like Jesus. And oh—by the way—they are all Muslim.

In the bubble we come from in the West, we can't even begin to envision what our Syrian neighbors who have been displaced have gone through. It would be arrogant to think we truly could, but let's use our imaginations for a minute.

I want you to picture your home. You are sitting on the porch or patio, it's a nice spring day, and your kids are playing in the yard with their neighbor friends. As you enjoy your favorite craft beer, green smoothie, or whatever trendy beverage you drink, you notice an odd humming in the air. It progressively gets louder, and you're curious, but not alarmed. You look up and see some odd looking, kind of eerie white planes in the distant sky. "Strange," you think. You know where I'm going . . .

In an instant your world stops. There is no sound but a ringing in your ears. As you look around everything is in slow motion; your street surreally appears to have transformed into a post-apocalyptic horror film. Disoriented, you look for your young children and spot them on the road, staring down at a red pool. As you run over, the closer you get, the more you can make out the figure in the red pool on the ground; it's the neighbor boy, his leg is severed, blood is everywhere, but he is conscious.

He holds his small arms out, you see deadening fear in his eyes as you run over to grab him, try to do anything you can, but what can you really do? You pick him up, blood pouring everywhere as your own children stand in shock, watching their friend helplessly bleed out. You look for a safe place to turn, someone to help you, but your world is vacant, there is no one, and his small, tender body goes limp in your hands.

This is only the beginning. This scene becomes your norm, and there is nothing to do but flee everything you have ever known. But even then, where will you go? There are many outside your nation who have the means to help, but they withhold their aid. They think helping you and your people survive would be too big of an inconvenience. There are places you can go to find some sort of refuge, but they require being locked up in a tent camp, and you have heard the horror stories of the sex traffickers who flock to the camps. It could be incredibly dangerous, especially for your children, who have already lost their childhood. You could try to find safety in a neighboring country, bypassing the camps, but then you would not be allowed to work—how would you survive? Your reality becomes a sort of darkness as far as you can see.

You see, our refugee neighbors go through scenarios like this and even worse regularly. No matter how much empathy we try to employ, we can't truly understand their pain.

Knowing all of this, imagine walking up to the door of a family who has recently lived through the unimaginable. You know this family has lost everything in a horrific manner and has every right to be angry with the world. I mean, we probably would be, right?

However, as you knock on the door, you are immediately warmly embraced with smiles and hugs from children and kisses from women, all of whom have never met you. You walk into their single room home furnished with only a few cushions and are immediately brought tea when you know they can't afford food for the month or the rent for these cold concrete floors.

These beautiful people lovingly embrace you—a stranger—with literally everything they have, even when they have almost nothing. You see, they are the embodiment of that widow Jesus praised, who had very little but gave anyway. They embody generous love. We Westerners who struggle to be generous out of our abundance have a lot to learn about the red-letter love ways of Jesus.

When Jesus says to love others, it looks like welcoming strangers into your home with kindness and tea. It means joyfully and generously giving freely out of the love in your heart, even when you have nothing yourself. It is genuine, it is kind, it is bold, and it has no other motive but pure love.

This is red-letter love, this is how we change our world, this is the point of following the ways of the true Messiah.

Chapter 3

HEY, NEIGHBOR

"And who is my neighbor?" an expert of religious law asked, looking for a loophole in that whole "love your neighbor" thing. I mean we know we are to love God and love our neighbor as ourselves, but who are we talking about here? Well, there are all the people in our clan, we tend to think of them as our neighbor. You know, the people who look, think, and act like us. The people we "do life with." Those are the people we would be okay with trying to love as we love ourselves or close to it, at least.

But they are the easiest to love, right?

In response to the question of who our neighbor is, Jesus, who I like to imagine could have been kind of a smart-ass—in a totally loving manner of course—told one of my favorite parables of all times: the parable of the Good Samaritan (Luke 10:25–37).

To the Jews listening to Jesus' story, Samaritans were the hated outsiders. We've already imagined this story as if we were in the role of the Samaritan, helping a wounded ISIS leader we are confident hates us. Let's now put ourselves in the shoes of Jesus's listeners and imagine now that we American Christians are the ones in need of help.

So Joel Osteen or some other American Christian televangelist type asks Jesus, "Well, the law says I am to love God and love my neighbor, but who is my neighbor, Jesus?"

Jesus responds, "A white, Christian, U.S. Army vet was traveling by train from Washington D.C. to New York City when he was attacked by robbers at a train station. The robbers stripped the guy, took all of his clothes, beat the crap out of him, and left him naked, bloody, and half dead. A Franklin Graham type happened to also be at the train station on his way to NYC; on his way to board, he saw the bloody naked guy and was super grossed out. So, carefully and somewhat annoyed, he walked around the man to get to his train. Next a good ol' Bible belt preacher with a big ol' King James Version Bible in hand came through to catch a train. He also saw the naked dude oozing blood and walked carefully around him, saying a quick prayer, of course, before catching his train.

"Finally, a Muslim refugee from Iraq whose wife and children had been murdered by an American drone strike, a man who also happened to be the cousin of an ISIS leader, came through and saw the soldier. When he saw the blood-covered, naked man struggling to breathe, he felt overwhelming compassion. He took some clothes out of his bag and helped the barely conscious man dress. He called an ambulance and rode with the man to a nearby hospital. Upon arrival, the Muslim man found that the wounded vet was without insurance, so he pulled out his credit card and took financial responsibility for all of the man's medical bills. Before the Muslim refugee man left, he instructed the nurse to make sure the man was taken well care of and to call him with any other needs or expenses.

So, Mr. Osteen, which of these three do you think was a neighbor to the military man who was robbed?

Joel, annoyed as hell, mumbled, "I guess the guy who had mercy on him."

And Jesus said, "Go and do the same."

And then Joel finally yet reluctantly opened his mega church to allow refuge for hurricane victims who had lost everything. Just kidding; that's a different story.

The point is, in his parable, Jesus made the person commonly seen as the enemy or outsider the hero. It was the "other" who showed mercy and love while those who would have been thought to be the wounded man's "people" avoided him, leaving him for dead. Jesus humanized "the other," the supposed enemy. He then told the religious elites to go and do the same. As in, go love your enemy, like the Samaritan (or ISIS affiliate)—your enemy—did in this parable.

How often do we do this individually? How often do we see most of American Christianity even attempt to love those who hate us? Can you imagine how the world would change if we extended this sort of kindness not only to our loved ones, but also to those who are the "other," those who make us feel uncomfortable, those who we think hate us or who we don't understand? To truly be the change in our broken world, truly trying to love the other is a task we have to embrace.

* * *

I want to tell you about my dear friend who truly lives out the Great Commandment of Jesus like no one I have ever seen.

My friend happens to be a refugee in the Middle East where he and his beautiful family live in an incredibly old refugee camp that looks more like cement apartment complexes than the tent camps you see on the news. It's kind of like a unique sort of small neighborhood.

Except that this "neighborhood" is partially surrounded by a massive—internationally deemed illegal—wall that cuts through their country's land. And this is not a normal wall. It hovers over the camp, twenty-six feet of concrete intimidation. The wall is complete with security cameras, motion control sensors, and multiple watch towers staffed 24/7 with the finest snipers. It feels as if you are in an open-air prison. So maybe unique is the wrong word, it is more like a small neighborhood you might see in a bad, chilling sci-fi movie.

Another fun (and by fun, I mean terrifying) fact about where my friend lives: there are often night raids that can occur at any given moment. What exactly is a night raid? Well, soldiers from the neighboring country (those sniper guys and some of their friends) storm in with their big guns, fingers always clasping the trigger, search random houses, and make arrests—often of young boys who are still just children.

Sometimes, the streets are filled with tear gas and gunfire. Want to resist? It may cost you your life or maybe just a few years in prison. Children, too. Years of prison for children. Let that sink in for a moment.

One summer, my husband and I were visiting our dear friends and were awakened by the gunfire of these soldiers. The next morning, our friends informed us that two young men had been shot. They themselves had spent the night in their young daughters' room, as they often did, shielding them on the floor. You never know how bad it can get at any moment.

This is not an out-of-the-ordinary event for them. Do you have children? Can you imagine spending regular nights sleeping on the floor to try to keep your children safe from stray bullets? You see, my friends live under mass oppression, apartheid. Their oppressors treat and look at them as subhuman. They live in daily fear as they are the enemy to a foreign nation on their own land. Like every person who faces some sort of oppression, my friend longs for equality. He longs to see his children grow up in peace.

I don't know about you, but it would be incredibly difficult for me not to be filled with bitterness against my oppressors. I mean really, my friend is more than justified to feel anger and a desire to retaliate, right? He lives in the midst of a true fear of a very real enemy.

However, my friend is an amazing soul, a far better person than I. One night, as we sat on a rooftop in conversation, he said to us, "I look at the faces of the young soldiers and I feel for them, I see they feel fear as we do. We are all human. If we could just share our stories with each other we could see our humanity, we could overcome the hate."

My friend chooses to humanize those who dehumanize him. He chooses to employ empathy when most of us would find it close to impossible to do so. And when there is no rational logic to choose love, he loves anyway.

My friend is the most welcoming, humble, kind person I have ever had the honor to know. He doesn't see his enemy as an enemy; he sees a fellow human and he loves boldly. The way he lives his life looks more like the ways of Jesus than any American Christian I have ever encountered. In the self-proclaimed "Christian Nation" of the world, we could learn so much about the ways of love from this Middle Eastern refugee man (go figure).

To be honest, the American White-Jesus Church tends to suck majorly at loving "the other." Our nation seems to be gripped with a constant fear of fabricated threats that inhibit us from loving while my friend loves even while enduring true oppression. While our nation fearfully closes its doors to those in need, he welcomes everyone he meets with open, gracious arms. Which sounds more like the ways of Jesus?

Instead of arguing fear-based justifications for why we can't be loving toward certain people, we can set a higher standard, one rooted in love and humanity. Let us learn from my friend, turn our backs on fear, and unify in love.

Let's be real, for the White-Jesus Church, Jesus' Great Commandment to love our enemy is more of a cute saying or loose guideline with a million ways around it. But Jesus was pretty direct as he said,

> "But I say to you that listen, Love your enemies, do good to those who hate you, bless those who curse you, pray for those who abuse you. If anyone strikes you on the cheek, offer the other also; and from anyone who takes away your coat do not withhold even your shirt. Give to everyone who begs from you; and if anyone takes away your goods, do not ask for them again. Do to others as you would have them do to you.
>
> "If you love those who love you, what credit is that to you? For even sinners love those who love them. If you do good to those who do good to you, what credit is that to you? For even sinners do the

same. If you lend to those from whom you hope to receive, what credit is that to you? Even sinners lend to sinners, to receive as much again. But love your enemies, do good, and lend, expecting nothing in return. Your reward will be great, and you will be children of the Most High; for he is kind to the ungrateful and the wicked. Be merciful, just as your Father is merciful."

Luke 6:27–36

So are we merciful to our deemed enemy? Do we give to anyone without expecting in return? Let's be real, the White-Jesus Church tends to love those who look, act, tithe, and believe as they do. Those who differ in any sense are labeled an enemy that is to be feared, judged, attacked, and condemned.

LGBTQ+ folk looking for a wedding cake—enemy. The "liberal agenda" to you know, actually take care of the vulnerable in our nation—enemy. Rap music—enemy. *Teen Vogue*—enemy. Immigrant seeking a better life—enemy. Refugee who has lost everything simply seeking safety for their children—enemy. I could go on for days, but I'm sure you get the point.

The ideology of the American White-Jesus has managed to label a million people groups as the enemy. Do they then—I don't know—follow the ways of their Savior as to how to react toward "your enemy"? Are we good to them, even if we think they are threatening us? Are we generous with them, even when we expect nothing in return?

Well, the White-Jesus Church campaigned pretty strongly to put an egocentric, bigoted, racist sexual predator in office as "leader" of this country in hopes that he would do things like build a literal wall and deport immigrants trying desperately to give their kids a better life, take health care away from millions of people, and even change who gets bathroom rights.

According to Pew Research, there is also the fact that 76 percent of white evangelical Christians supported a Muslim ban.[1] In the midst of one of the greatest humanitarian crises of our lifetime, with millions—like the man in the story of the Good Samaritan—wounded and in desperate need of refuge, the White-Jesus Church has crossed to the other side of the road. People say that we need to look out for "us" first, that we can't just allow anyone in who is hurting and needs safety because they might actually hurt *us* and threaten *our* safety. We need to make sure we take care of our own shallow desires and warped perception of security above the life of others. It's as if not only are we ignoring the Great Commandment of our Savior, we are deliberately contradicting it and even campaigning to hurt the "other" for a perceived self-centered gain.

Why do we do this? If we gained the whole world by taking care of ourselves first, if we achieved all of the personal status, wealth, and success we could dream of, if we could make our own lives perfect, what good is any of it if we lose our soul (Mark 8:36)?

* * *

The first trip my husband and I took to the Syrian border together was a few months after our wedding; it was pretty much our honeymoon trip. We spent a couple of weeks at the Syrian border in Jordan and then headed over to Palestine—a place we both love—to finish up our unconventionally awesome honeymoon.

Now if you have ever made the trek from Jordan to Palestine, you understand the intensity. It was two crazy, near-death cab rides through the twisting roads of Jordan, an hour-or-two long bus trip (just crossing the easily walkable short bridge into the West Bank), multiple Israeli check points filled with teenagers whose index fingers constantly caressed the triggers of their AK-47s, and a long-ass line in the blistering heat before we arrived at Israeli customs to get our visas to get into the West Bank. After some bad coffee and a few hours of waiting, due to some natural questioning of my husband's Iraqi visas in his passport, we were finally granted access to the beautiful land that is Palestine.

Stepping outside the desert customs building into basically the middle of nowhere, we were greeted by a few eager Israeli taxi drivers trying to sway us, like we were in a used car lot, into taking a taxi to Jerusalem for the low, low price of "150 American dollars." The drive is like half an hour, so $150 is insane, and I had no desire to waste money getting ripped off that could be used for something more practical, like *kanafeh* (that is, the most amazing pastry in this universe).

Being the natural (often obsessive) problem solver that I tend to be, I scanned the street and noticed a variety of large buses. So, I naturally asked the Israeli taxi drivers if there was a bus we could take. To our disappointment, the men informed us there were no buses that would be available for us. Then I spotted a bus ticket booth with strictly Arabic writing. Destinations including Jericho, Bethlehem, Jerusalem, Ramallah, etc. After years of studying Arabic in college, thank God I at least picked up on how to read the language, even if I can barely speak it.

I nudged my husband and we thanked the men and

let them know we were going to check out the Palestinian buses. And then we heard:

"You can't take *those buses*, it is *very dangerous*! You don't know what it is like there!" The main taxi driver exclaimed rather dramatically.

To which my husband responded sharply, "We know exactly what it is like there."

We have both spent time in Palestine and hold a deep love for the people and country. The man's attempt at invoking a fabricated fear caused an ache of deep frustration in both of us. So we headed over to get our bus tickets, for the equivalent of $15 USD, to Jericho and then another $10 USD for a taxi from Jericho to our final destination, Aida Refugee Camp in Bethlehem.

We boarded the half-full bus and every eye shot up at us, and honestly, it took me off guard. I confess, I did feel a little intimidated. I thought, "Are we that rare of a presence on the Palestinian bus route? Are typical Westerners really so irrationally fearful that they are totally cool with being drastically ripped off taking a cab?"

So, with all eyes on us, we smiled and took a seat. A man in front of us dropped his cigarettes. As my husband quickly picked them up, he smiled, and a conversation sparked.

"Welcome to Palestine!" said the man who was headed home to Hebron, after he asked where we were from. Quickly, another young couple smiled, introducing themselves and also welcomed us and invited us to share their cab with us when we got to the bus station.

When we arrived at the crowded bus station in Jericho we went through Palestinian customs, again the only non-Arabs in the vicinity. As we walked into a place in the West Bank that our society tells us we should fear, we were welcomed with grand smiles and kindness like we would never experience in the U.S. One of the custom officers (who had seriously awesome hair, like David Hasselhoff, circa 1986) even jumped up and left his post, insisting on helping us find a good cab and getting our luggage situated.

As we sat amongst a couple hundred people, all of us waiting for our ride, I thought, I am "supposed" to be afraid to be here. I am "supposed" to fear people who are fully embracing me with genuine kindness, going out of their way to welcome and help me in a way that I have never experienced domestically. We are so concerned with our warped perception of safety that we easily dehumanize an entire region based on irrational, fear-invoking rumors when the reality is, we could learn a lot from the vast kindness found in places like Palestine. Loving like the red-letter Jesus means pursuing the path of loving our enemy boldly with deep kindness, embracing love instead of fear.

We were clearly the "other." No one we encountered on our trek had to show us kindness. The fact that we come from a country that strongly backs their oppressors gives them every right to label us Americans as the enemy. How often do we stereotype and fear one another even at home?

In all honesty, if a Muslim woman walks out of an airport, really anywhere in the U.S., how many White-Jesus Christians would independently approach this stranger out of kindness and hospitality? Do you think many of them would even speak to her (aside from handing out tracts)?

Our Muslim Palestinian neighbors chose to show us love. Their simple embrace looked far more like the ways of Jesus, the Good Samaritan, loving their enemy as themselves, than what we tend to see in the Western ideology of White-Jesus Christianity.

Loving our neighbor—including the one considered our enemy—is completely countercultural in our society. To step outside of our comfort zone to be kind to a stranger may feel completely awkward, but it can start with something small. Mother Teresa, who was definitely a pro at loving others, said, "The smile is the beginning of love." Love can be sparked by something as simple as a smile from the heart. A bold, underrated action that even the most introverted of us can do with ease. Seriously, try it. Smile at someone who society teaches you to fear. Do it enough and something will change inside your own heart. If we all did it enough, something would change within our whole world.

Chapter 4
SELLING TICKETS TO HEAVEN

Jesus was definitely not a "do as I say, not as I do" sort of guy. He lived his life on the commandment of radical love and instructed his followers to do the same. This ideology was central to the ways of the real, red-letter Jesus. Now White-Jesus, on the other hand, has a bit of a different focus. White-Jesus tends to focus more on what we call the Great Commission, which has become central to the ideology of much of the modern American Church. I say the "modern" American Church because the term "Great Commission" wasn't coined until the seventeenth century by Dutch missionary Justinian von Welz. It was not until the nineteenth century that British mega missionary to China, Hudson Taylor, popularized the term and pushed the idea that all Christians have an obligation or *commission* to convert others to Christianity.[1]

The Great Commission is based on a few verses at the end of the Gospel of Matthew. Jesus had recently bounced back from the darkness of death or wherever he was, and his boys—the eleven (because Judas made bad choices)—went to Galilee to some mountains where Jesus had told them to go. When they got there and saw Jesus, alive and not in a zombie form, they were like "this is so crazy," and they worshiped him. That's when Jesus said what is now called the Great Commission:

"Go therefore and make disciples of all nations, baptizing them in the name of the Father and of the Son
and of the Holy Spirit, and teaching them to obey
everything that I have commanded you. And remember that I am with you always, to the end of the age."
Matt. 28:19–20

It's the "go and make disciples" part that tends to be
translated as a command to convert people to Christianity
and has been elevated to a place where the goal of conversion has overpowered even the Great Command.

I often overhear pastors and church groups at coffee shops talking about "unreached" people groups in the
"10/40 window," the area between 10 and 40 degrees
north latitude where a huge percentage of the world's non-
Christian (and non-white) people live—North Africa, the
Middle East, India, China, and Southeast Asia. These pastors brag about all the people they convinced to "say the
prayer" that week. It's as if they are holding this strategizing
meeting to figure out how they can most successfully convert whomever and convince them of the "truth" that they
hold. This ingrained ideology tends to look like a numbers
game. The goal is to "save" (convert) as many souls as possible, and then maybe you win or something—I am honestly
not quite sure what—maybe points in heaven? Or maybe a
mansion in heaven. When I was about eight years old, I went
through a tornado phase where I wanted to be a meteorolo-
gist and chase tornadoes (yeah, I watched *Twister* a few too
many times). I remember hearing something about everyone
getting to have a mansion in heaven, and I would imagine
my mansion to be made of glass or diamonds and shaped
like a tornado—yep, that was my dream house. So maybe if
you get enough points you can get your "dream mansion."

In all seriousness, the conversion goal looks like an odd competition, and its players are often aggressive and uncomfortable to be around. I imagine these Christians having conversations with the non-Christians they want to convert, sitting there not listening but waiting for any chance to strategically insert their beliefs. It's uncomfortable; it's not how normal people have a conversation. For those uncomfortable with face-to-face evangelism, there are even tracts that on first appearance look like money, but upon closer inspection say something like, "The life of Jesus is more precious than any amount of money, and if you choose to accept him into your heart, you can save yourself from hellfire." I worked at a restaurant back in the day and, no joke, we had people leave these tracts as tips.

There are different types of players, but the game is the same. The shared message is something like, "I want to save your soul, and in order to save your soul from eternal hellfire where there is gnashing of teeth, you need to accept Jesus Christ as your Lord and personal Savior by saying these magic words to God." The end, points received. It's like a get-out-of-hell-free card that completely misses the larger and far greater purpose of following the ways of Jesus, here, in our lives today.

Now, please don't misunderstand me—I'm not saying you should never talk about your faith. I really like Jesus, and I talk about him because trying to follow his ways is a big part of my life and I think he's a badass. However, I never ever talk about Jesus with the agenda to convert anyone. Awkwardly inserting your religious ideals or straight up arguing why people need Jesus so they don't go to hell is creepy and morbid—and frankly, not at all what Jesus intended!

Consider first, what exactly did Jesus mean by "go make disciples"? Why do we assume it means to convert people to Christianity? There was no such thing as "Christianity" until a few hundred years after his death. Did we ever see Jesus spending his time trying to convert people to a religion? A disciple is a follower, someone who learns and tries to implement the teachings of a master. If that wasn't clear, Jesus laid it out more specifically, saying "and teach them to obey all that I have commanded." Teach them to obey what he has commanded. Okay, so what did he command? Was there any sort of "great" commandment that Jesus specifically gave?

Yeah, we all know where I am going. Jesus commanded them to love others as Jesus had loved them. We know what he commanded. There isn't a question here. Really, what we call the Great Commission would seem more like an instruction to teach people the Great Commandment.

What if instead of focusing so much on how we can convert others, we focused all that energy on how we can love bolder like Jesus? What if we sat in coffee shops and had meetings to try to figure out how to love our neighbors better? Fortunately, there are, in fact, real-life people out there focusing on how to better love others. They are the ones changing the world (and, on top of it all, people actually like hanging out with them).

* * *

Years ago, after I discovered that Jesus was cool but I was still super green in trying to figure out this whole following him thing, I went to a class on "missions" at a church that I thought was trustworthy. I generally wasn't ridiculously naive, but for some reason I thought it would be a class more on like, humanitarian efforts and loving people.

They had all these "experts" and fancy people talking, and they showed us this video about "unreached" people groups, emphasizing the "10/40 window," the supposed area where "poor people of those regions have the least access to the gospel." We watched a little promo film, they gave us pamphlets, and then one of those fancy people spoke. I sat uncomfortably in my hard church chair and listened intently as this person basically said that if these people don't get access to the gospel they will go to hell. I'm sure my facial expression was blatantly obvious, but it just seemed ridiculous; it felt as if these people would be serving Kool-Aid soon.

After the class was over I stuck around to talk to one of the "experts." It went something like this:

"Hi, I'm Sheri and I just had a few questions if that is okay with you?"

"Well of course, dear," the expert Christian said with a big smile. (I added the "dear"; it was more implied by tone, if you know what I mean.)

"Soooooo . . . are you saying that if those who are Christians don't go and tell people who are not Christians about Jesus, and those non-Christians die, that they are going to go to hell?" I asked with a genuine are-you-serious type of confusion.

Caught off guard and a bit uncomfortable, the expert said with less of a smile, "Well, to go to heaven you have to accept Jesus as your Savior, and if people never hear about Jesus they will never know about the good news and wouldn't be able to accept Jesus and therefore wouldn't go to heaven."

"So you are telling me that if we don't try to go and persuade foreign villages in Africa to accept our belief system, God sends them to hell?"

"The Bible does say the only way to heaven is through proclaiming Jesus Christ as your Savior."

"Okay, this is definitely some Kool-Aid level crap," I thought as I left, baffled by what I had just heard. To be honest, the idea felt ridiculously arrogant. Why would people think that God needs them to "save" others? At the time, I was ignorant to the fact that what this "expert" was saying is actually pretty mainstream theology. Jesus did say, "I am the way, and the truth, and the life. No one comes to the Father except through me" (John 14:6). People latch on to this verse and insist that if we don't tell people that Jesus is the only way, God will have no other option but to send them to an eternity of hell fire. Except, let's be real, this line of thinking sounds nothing like the radically loving way of Jesus. This line of thinking sounds like self-elevation, making ourselves the hero, not practicing sacrificial love. We are not meant to be little messiahs, and in our attempts to "save" souls, we are actually putting ourselves on a pedestal, which effectively dehumanizes others.

Let us ponder Christian ministries for a moment. Basically, these ministries tend to consist of like-minded folk with a heart for fill-in-the-blank causes in which they are trying to help a need. A lot of churches have programs to assist refugees; there is a definite need and it's trendy right now. We see ministries that do things like offer ESL classes and help new arrivals furnish their homes and navigate their new communities. All helpful things, right? The answer is yes, these are very helpful and needed things. But for some, there is often an ulterior motive: helping with clear physical needs while hoping to address what you perceive as their spiritual needs. The reality is that if the underlying reasons you decide to form a relationship with someone is to "enlighten" them, whether you want to admit it to yourself or not, they become a project. To view a person as a project—something for you to essentially fix or save—is dehumanizing to its core. You are putting yourself on a pedestal trying to impart your "truth and knowledge." It is a repackaged manifest destiny mentality. This sort of ideology dehumanizes "the other," and it has led to really hurtful actions and policies that have been supported by the majority of evangelical Christians, so we need to ask some hard questions.

How can so many of those who claim Christianity run all these seemingly wonderful ministries to help others and in the same breath advocate and justify policies aimed at hurting the very people we claim to be trying to help? Why would so many White-Jesus American Christians support a ban on immigrants and refugees from primarily Muslim-majority countries, for example, or hold a belief that all Muslims are terrorists?

While sitting in a café in southern Iraq, an Iraqi man in his mid-thirties told my husband that during the war in Iraq, the U.S. would bomb their cities, sometimes killing their friends and family; then shortly after, white people would walk around handing out Bibles trying to "save their souls." Having people from the very nation that is wiping out your neighborhood come and try to "save your soul," because you may be killed by one of their nation's drone strikes, seems like some serious hypocrisy and a very unhealthy "savior" complex.

I once was doing some humanitarian work overseas and I met a woman who had come separately with a Christian organization to help and do some sort of extended mission trip type thing. We were working in a Muslim country and the young woman, no joke, said, "I hate these people—Muslims." A friend of mine asked her why she was even there, to which she replied, "I didn't have a choice; the organization sends us wherever they want."

The next day, in the morning before distributing food, water, and other necessary supplies, the same full-grown adult woman obnoxiously asked, "When can I share a story about Jesus to these people?"

That was why she was there. Straight-up conversion. She didn't even like the people. She was playing that weird numbers game, and thinking she was fulfilling the Great Commission. But she was selling tickets to heaven, not making disciples. How can you make disciples of Jesus, teaching them his Great Command to love others, without following the Great Command yourself? Trying to convert someone is not loving them. No matter how much you say it is, it's just not.

Jesus came not to be served, but to serve. Trying to follow the ways of Jesus means putting ourselves beneath others, not in the humble, bragging kind of way, but with a willingness to sacrifice our wants and even needs to love others as Jesus did. We can't whitewash the radical calling of Jesus. To truly find life we must be willing to lose it. Lose the status, lose the agenda, lose the control, lose our ego, lose the "game."

Imagine what our world could look like if instead of living a burdensome life attempting to "save" souls, we poured all that effort into simply loving others—straight up—without an underlying motive. This sort of red-letter love would leave an imprint so deep on this world that once you get a glimpse, you could never turn back because there is no truer purpose. It's not glamorous to love without expectations, without the gratification of the praise you get from those who look and think like you. The question you have to ask yourself is, do you want to follow the wide path while clinging to the comforts and securities of your world, or do you want to follow the narrow path that aligns with the Great Command of Jesus?

We need a revolution of love in our world, and where else are we going to learn how to do that? YouTube? I doubt it. We need to follow the example of the one who taught us how to love in a revolutionary, countercultural way—the radical, refugee Messiah.

Chapter 5

MORE HUMBLE THAN YOU WOULD THINK

I feel pretty safe in saying that of all Jesus' wonderful characteristics, the hardest one for Americans to emulate is his humility. Let's be honest, we are not the best at being humble. Our nation is not exactly known for being an unpretentious people. Real humility is so lacking in our culture and likewise in White-Jesus Christianity, that when we do see it, it stands out, mesmerizing in its beauty.

Think about it: Jesus was the Messiah, and if anyone would be entitled to living a life of ordering ten chocolate chip cookies with medium-sized chips and none too close to the center, it would have been him. But J wasn't about that life of privilege. He didn't have a diva bone in his body. To the contrary, unlike the "big deal" religious folk in both our time and his, he didn't come to be served—he came to serve.

Humility is not about putting ourselves down. What it really comes down to is simply putting others first—above ourselves. Really there is not a lot that embodies love more than elevating others. Point blank.

Jesus said, "The greatest among you will be your servant. All who exalt themselves will be humbled, and all who humble themselves will be exalted" (Matt. 23:11–12). That is the kind of life that Jesus talked about and lived.

I don't know about you, but the most life-giving humans I have ever encountered are those who I have felt were a "big deal," but they were more interested in encouraging me and others than standing around talking about how awesome they were. They *were* awesome, and I personally would have been all good if they had just talked about their awesomeness. I think Glennon Doyle embodies this point better than anyone. Though I have never actually met her in real life, as far as I can tell, she doesn't seem to use her status to self-inflate her own ego; she uses her privilege to focus on loving others. For example, Glennon is pretty much A-list—I mean, she is buddies with Oprah—but she takes the time to reply to comments on her social media in a genuinely kind and encouraging manner. Definitely not something you see every day. She has focused her success on encouraging us all to be warriors of love, to love "the other" in big ways without discounting the change that we ourselves can make in this world. That's humility—elevating others over ourselves. That's the way of the red letters.

Think about the people who have impacted your journey the most with a manner of encouragement. Are they more into themselves or do they put others first? You very likely may have never asked yourself this question, but I bet the answer is obvious.

Jesus embodied humility both boldly and subtly; it was engrained in how he lived. There is one story in particular where Jesus portrays an act of humility in a manner that could be seen as socially uncomfortable—not just because feet freak me out a bit—but also because the message of elevating others above oneself is so incredibly raw.

Now before the festival of the Passover, Jesus knew that his hour had come to depart from this world and go to the Father. Having loved his own who were in the world, he loved them to the end.

The devil had already put it into the heart of Judas son of Simon Iscariot to betray him. And during supper Jesus, knowing that the Father had given all things into his hands, and that he had come from God and was going to God, got up from the table, took off his outer robe, and tied a towel around himself. Then he poured water into a basin and began to wash the disciples' feet and to wipe them with the towel that was tied around him.

He came to Simon Peter, who said to him, "Lord, are you going to wash my feet?" Jesus answered, "You do not know now what I am doing, but later you will understand." Peter said to him, "You will never wash my feet." Jesus answered, "Unless I wash you, you have no share with me." Simon Peter said to him, "Lord, not my feet only but also my hands and my head!"

Jesus said to him, "One who has bathed does not need to wash, except for the feet, but is entirely clean. And you are clean, though not all of you." For he knew who was to betray him; for this reason he said, "Not all of you are clean."

After he had washed their feet, had put on his robe, and had returned to the table, he said to them, "Do you know what I have done to you? You call me Teacher and Lord—and you are right, for that is what I am. So if I, your Lord and Teacher, have washed your feet, you also ought to wash one another's feet. For I have set you an example that you also should do as I have done to you."

John 13:1–15

Let me put this into a bit more perspective. Back in the days when people only wore sandals and there were no pedicures (as far as I know), walking about the terrain of Palestine, and eating in a position where everyone has a front row ticket to your dirty and probably smelly feet, feet washing was a normative practice. The job of foot washer generally was that of the lowliest of servants. It wasn't a glamorous job by any manner. Regardless, Jesus, the great teacher of these guys, the guy the disciples admired more than anyone who had ever existed, stripped down and took their dirty feet into his hands and cleansed them.

As you can see from Peter's response, the raw humility Jesus was showing made the disciples uncomfortable with the overwhelming and knowingly undeserved reversal of status, elevating them by lowering himself to the role of servant. To be real with everyone, I can't imagine how unworthy I would feel at this gesture, but I also bet that I would also feel incredibly loved. Furthermore, Jesus made it a point to instruct his disciples to follow his example, to serve others above themselves as Jesus had done throughout his time with them.

You see Jesus, aka the Messiah, saw himself not as the supreme hero of the universe but as a servant to both God and those who surrounded him, many of whom he humbly served regardless of the fact that society would have had nothing to do with them. Of course, people in mainstream society tend to be exclusive jerks.

Can you imagine what impact we could have on this world if we consciously worked to humbly serve and love others first, to elevate the status of others above our own arrogant egos?

While I've met a few of those amazingly other-focused

people here in the U.S., I don't think it was until I experienced the humility of our friends in the Middle East that I started to realize how beautiful and important this trait is. Unlike here in the U.S., elevating others is built into the culture of the Middle East. It is not uncommon to meet a total stranger in the Middle East and be immediately invited over for the best dinner of your life. Drinking tea and having meaningful, not-rushed conversations are a way of life. Hospitality and community are emphasized in the region over individual traits—and there is so much we could learn from that.

Here are some things that I have learned through being around some of these amazing humans:

Humility is kind to the other, the stranger, the marginalized.

Humility listens first. It has that slow to speak, quick to listen sort of swagger.

Humility is not self-loathing in any manner, it is simply letting go of our massive egos and elevating others.

Humility smiles at people: strangers in the grocery store, the family down the street who recently moved to the U.S. and who speak a different language, the young pregnant girl walking to school, the other.

Humility changes our souls and other's in amazingly profound ways.

What if instead of driving past a homeless person with a cardboard sign, we stopped and invited them into our home for a meal? What if instead of "protecting" ourselves from the perceived risk of international terrorists, we opened our doors to refugees? What if instead of condemning the girl at Planned Parenthood, we offered her our hand? What if instead of waiting for our turn to speak, we stopped to listen?

What if instead of being obsessed with ourselves, we focused on elevating others in love? What could that look like in our world today?

* * *

I want to tell you a little story. My husband and I met through some mutual friends and connected through our love of Palestine. At the time, I was living and teaching in Houston and Rich's life was in Des Moines, where Monsanto corn is king, and there are more pigs than people.

Before we met in what I call real life, we connected and started talking on the phone. We both had similar passions and some other things in common, so talking on the phone some nights turned into talking on the phone pretty much every night, which eventually turned into awkward video chats because we are both too old for things like FaceTiming.

Now, if you would have asked me ten years ago where my top five places that I had no interest in ever traveling to, ever, Iowa definitely would have been on that list. I mean c'mon, I'm from Houston, the most diverse city in the U.S. with a larger population than every city/town/hamlet in Iowa combined. Iowa really didn't stand out as a cool place to me.

Rich is the kind of guy who can be super confident and incredibly charming. And like most youngish men, maybe even sometimes a little too confident about things that don't really matter, if you know what I mean. When we started talking, Rich pretty much always mentioned something about how great Des Moines was. "Des Moines has a great art scene, there are a lot of young people, there's this super cool music festival and an awesome T-shirt store called Ray Gun, we have really good corn, etc." Being from a massive city, in all honesty I was like, "Okay, this guy really likes his city and oh my gosh, he brags about it a lot. I wonder if he hasn't been to many 'real cities.'" Don't get me wrong, my husband is amazing, but he could be a bit too arrogant regarding Des Moines-flipping-Iowa. Mind you he was "selling" Des Moines for a reason, but really, his confidence is on a level where he thinks—I mean knows— that he's awesome. Some could say at times that he may come off as a bit cocky. So, before we met in person, I knew Rich was an amazing guy, but I questioned how humble he was; I mean, he *always* had a cool story—you know the type.

Regardless, eventually, after selling the crap out of Des Moines, he convinced me to visit for a week. Now let's be real, it wasn't because Rich made Des Moines sound so amazing that I decided to check out the capital of the middle of nowhere. I was teaching and it was my summer break, and so I decided f-it and agreed to come up for a week and hang out with this really awesome guy with an awesome beard. And when I came up, I was seriously blown away. Not just because Des Moines actually is a pretty cool city, but because this guy had an entire week of incredibly thoughtful dates planned out. I have never met anyone who made me feel as special as he did (and still does); it honestly felt like some Disney movie crap.

Yes, he can have the tendency to brag a bit—but he also has an incredible, unnaturally natural ability to put others first. He is incredibly thoughtful and the most respectful man I have ever encountered. I know people say this all the time about their partner, but I seriously did not think guys like this existed. One time he brought me Thelma's—the most amazing ice cream cookie sandwiches, which I fell in love with in Iowa— to Texas on a plane, all rigged up in his carry-on with ice packs and everything. Don't act like that's not pretty damn impressive.

But I'm not just talking about awesome dates and sweet gestures, I am talking about in everyday life and toward everyone he encounters.

For instance, the other day we were driving along and we saw a guy walking down the road in the fifteen-degree weather, wearing a T-shirt with his arms tucked in. My husband is that guy who literally turns the car around, takes his coat off, tracks the guy down at a gas station, and gives him his coat. And that is not the only time he has done something like this.

Nonprofits don't pay a ton, but even if he was broke, he would give anyone he sees with a cardboard sign all of the cash in his wallet. He is the kind of guy that, if he has it, he will give it away to love others. He will use his last sixty dollars to help the woman in front of him at the grocery store whose card gets denied. He quit a fancy job in medical sales making bank in order to be with his kids, then he quit another stable job to start a nonprofit focused on loving refugees from the Middle East and North Africa. He literally will give everything he has for a stranger and truly not want or expect anything in return.

Now, I know I am bragging about my husband quite a bit, but it amazes me how he always elevates the needs of others. This is true humility. True humility is not a lack of confidence or really even the counterbalance to some arrogance. Humility is loving others first, always. And really, most of us suck at this if we are being truly honest here.

Humility is beautiful, often subtle, yet radical selflessness.

A few years before my husband and I met, I wrote down five characteristics I would want in a man if I ever chose to date again (which I had zero desire to do at that time): intelligent, funny, kind, attractive, and humble. A couple of weeks before we got married, I found this list in some random "junk" drawer and it overwhelmed me how this guy met every single characteristic on this list with a bang. It was crazy and it humbled me immensely.

As I said earlier, humility is my favorite trait in a person.

Y'all, this is what loving others looks like; humility both vibrant and subtle can change our world. Remember what that radical refugee said? The first will be last and the last will be first. That's what Jesus did. That's the way of red-letter love.

* * *

Have you ever been to a party where you are surrounded by people you don't know and forced to engage in everyone's least favorite activity—small talk—and you notice something weird? The person you are talking to looks like they are actually paying attention to your awkward story about your cat, Bryzzo, and they are asking follow-up questions and everything like they care about what you are saying even though you are really just a couple of randos trying to be polite at an uncomfortable social gathering? The fact that this person isn't doing what most people do during small talk (eagerly waiting to talk about themselves) catches you off guard, and they aren't being creepy or insincere or anything, and oddly enough it honestly feels really refreshing.

This is the rare person in our ego-driven Western culture that practices true humility. It sounds super simple, right? They are just actively listening, but let's be real, most of our culture struggles severely with this skill. In a filtered world of social media and "reality" TV, most of us feed into the lie that to be liked by others (and whether you want to admit it or not, we all want others to like us on some level), we need to put on a show so that everyone can see how awesome we are and that will make them like us. It's about how we can manipulate a situation to give off the best possible appearance of ourselves.

The thing is, this course of action isn't going to attract people to us. It turns out that egocentrism is not actually an appealing quality.

We tend to naturally gravitate toward those with what we perceive as higher status in society. Movie stars, the Kardashians, Beyoncé, Anthony Rizzo of the Chicago Cubs, and so on. We get excited about meeting people with "status," people who we see as a big deal. For instance, a few weeks ago I met Bernie Sanders, and I was elated. I love the Bern. It was awesome. I got a picture with him and everything, which I of course made my Facebook profile pic right away.

But really, who cares? What did that change in the world? Nothing, really. And Jesus didn't operate that way. Jesus wasn't angling to meet Caesar, or even to cozy up to the most respected people in the neighborhood. Jesus sought out the young single mom who waitresses all night to get through college, the immigrant working three jobs to support his family, the refugee whose child is growing up knowing nothing but war. And why? Because Jesus understood that loving those the world loves does nothing, but loving the marginalized can change everything.

One day Jesus was passing through Jericho and there was a man "named Zacchaeus; he was a chief tax collector and was rich."

He was trying to see who Jesus was, but on account of the crowd he could not, because he was short in stature. So he ran ahead and climbed a sycamore tree to see him, because he was going to pass that way. When Jesus came to the place, he looked up and said to him, "Zacchaeus, hurry and come down; for I must stay at your house today." So he hurried down and was happy to welcome him. All who saw it began to grumble and said, "He has gone to be the guest of one who is a sinner." Zacchaeus stood there and said to the Lord, "Look, half of my possessions, Lord, I will give to the poor; and if I have defrauded anyone of anything, I will pay back four times as much." Then Jesus said to him, "Today salvation has come to this house, because he too is a son of Abraham. For the Son of Man came to seek out and to save the lost."

Luke 19:1–10

Back in the day, tax collectors were super sketch and almost always stole from people, so they were not well-liked by pretty much anyone. But Jesus, who was a big deal, saw Zacchaeus in his humanity—not his bad choices—and invited himself over to his house. Now when the people saw that he was going to a tax collector's house they were like, "Ew, he's going to the house of a sinner." But J didn't care, and because Jesus was humble enough to extend love to this guy that nobody liked much, Zacchaeus was changed and started to love others in big ways.

Y'all, humility is underrated, but it is a vital part of the way of Jesus, the way of red-letter love. To simply see people and put them before yourself, whether through grand actions like giving your car to a family who needs it more than you, or subtle actions like simply listening to the stories of the marginalized, are how we become the change. If we can start taking the time to truly see the other, we begin to find that humility can become part of our everyday lives.

Chapter 6
BLEEDING HEARTS
AND BOLD LOVE

Some of us are born hypersensitive to emotion and basically wired for empathy. You know, the bleeding-heart types. I definitely fall into the category of those who have the tendency to feel emotions more deeply and can be emotionally reactive in an impulsive manner (at least act surprised), but can also feel others' emotions as their own, not in like in a scary, spooky way, but in that deep empathy is hardwired within.

Whether or not you are an inherent empath, empathy is a trait we all have on some level. It is a skill that can take us out of our me-centered universe while forcing us to better understand the feelings of others.

Often we try to shut down our empathy skills, because feeling the pain of others can be, well, painful. In general, people don't tend to want to be heartbroken constantly, reading about the thousands of children who die from starvation each day as we throw half of our Chipotle burrito away.

Regardless of our efforts to avoid feelings of sadness or hurt, sometimes there are instances that catch us off guard, and empathy sneaks through our walls of purposeful ignorance that we try to hold strong. One of those times globally was when the world saw photos of the lifeless, limp body of three-year-old Aylan Kurdi washed onto the shore of a Turkish beach. Even now, I bet your heart hurts at the thought of this sweet small boy's needless death as his family, who had already lost everything due to war in their nation, desperately tried to find refuge and life somewhere in this world that had turned its back.

Though some hard empathy may sneak up on us in these sorts of cases, we have the tendency to disconnect as quickly as possible to the heart-wrenching feelings these photos may force upon us. We make ourselves busy, work overtime, go order our grande no-whip, almond milk, two-pump caramel latte, and then get upset about the color of the cup the barista hands us. We distract ourselves through many means.

The truth is that we have the choice to either embrace empathy or push it away.

Though it may "feel better" to stay ignorant, empathy is a vital precursor to compassion, and it will ultimately end in us actually having to do something ourselves to love those on the fringe, because that's what compassion does.

So maybe embracing some not-super-fun feelings could possibly be worth it?

You know, Jesus had some on-point empathy skills, and compassion was embedded into everything he did.

When he saw those who were physically or mentally sick, "he had compassion for them and cured their sick." (Matt. 14:14).

When he saw those who were emotionally hurting, he intervened:

> As he approached the gate of the town, a man who had died was being carried out. He was his mother's only son, and she was a widow; and with her was a large crowd from the town. When the Lord saw her, he had compassion for her and said to her, "Do not

weep." Then he came forward and touched the bier,
and the bearers stood still. And he said, "Young man,
I say to you, rise!" The dead man sat up and began to
speak, and Jesus gave him to his mother.

Luke 7:11–15

When he saw those who were hungry after they had been
listening to him for days, he met their needs:

> Jesus called his disciples to him and said, "I have
> compassion for the crowd, because they have been
> with me now for three days and have nothing to eat;
> and I do not want to send them away hungry, for
> they might faint on the way." The disciples said to
> him, "Where are we to get enough bread in the desert
> to feed so great a crowd?" Jesus asked them, "How
> many loaves have you?" They said, "Seven, and a
> few small fish." Then ordering the crowd to sit down
> on the ground, he took the seven loaves and the fish;
> and after giving thanks he broke them and gave them
> to the disciples, and the disciples gave them to the
> crowds. And all of them ate and were filled; and they
> took up the broken pieces left over, seven baskets
> full. Those who had eaten were four thousand men,
> besides women and children."
>
> Matt. 15:32–38

When he saw those who were lost in life, he took them
under his wing:

> The apostles gathered around Jesus, and told him
> all that they had done and taught. He said to them,
> "Come away to a deserted place all by yourselves and
> rest a while." For many were coming and going, and

they had no leisure even to eat. And they went away in the boat to a deserted place by themselves. Now many saw them going and recognized them, and they hurried there on foot from all the towns and arrived ahead of them. As he went ashore, he saw a great crowd; and he had compassion for them, because they were like sheep without a shepherd; and he began to teach them many things."

Mark 6:30–34

In every example above, Jesus' compassion led him to act. He showed deep love as he felt deep empathy. Compassion wasn't simply a forced or superficial response to the hurt that Jesus encountered; it was deeply embedded into his teachings and resulted in action. Jesus was well aware that the ability to feel for others is a vital component in the ability to sacrificially love others, especially when it comes to those outside your circle, those who are different than you.

How do we respond to the mess of hurt we see in our world? Are we looking away? Are we choosing ignorance over empathy and compassion?

What if instead of acting as if we are too busy or unable to truly help the hurting, we looked toward the way Jesus acted out of deep compassion. How he helped the physically and mentally sick, wept with the weeping, fed the hungry, and straight up never refused his hand to the vulnerable. The meaning of the word compassion is *to suffer with*. It's not going to be pleasant all the time. Jesus suffered with the other, so what if we choose to suffer with the other too?

* * *

Empathy can be grand or subtle; either way, it changes lives. A couple of months ago I went to an art exhibit showcasing pieces meant to be beautiful expressions of the brokenness that we see in our world, or something along those lines. Now, I like art in general, but I am not the kind of person who is majorly impacted by some yellow squares painted on a canvas. If you are, I admire your passion. Most pieces of art, I tend to enjoy looking at for about fifteen to thirty seconds tops, and then I am pretty much over it and need something new to stimulate my mind. There are only so many pictures of Mary and friends looking down at a chubby, white, naked baby Jesus that can hold my interest until I am over the whole theme.

So I was kind of bored and skeptical as I toured this little art museum in Des Moines and walked into that room full of art that was supposed to represent pain. There was one art piece that was like giant pieces of broken glass glued together, there were imprints of the cracks of the streets of Palestine, there was a dead baby horse (like a real-life, taxidermy baby horse), and all sorts of other things. So when I walked into this room and saw what looked like a metallic scarf nailed to the wall, I didn't even try to interpret or read the deeper meaning. It was a flipping scarf. I gave it barely a glance and headed over to seemingly more interesting pieces of brokenness.

As I was staring at what looked like a zillion black marbles in a perfect circle on the floor, my husband asked if I had checked out the scarf and told me I should take a look at it. Though I was pretty much mesmerized by the shiny black marbles that I promise looked way cooler than they sound, I reluctantly went over to take an actual look at this scarf.

As I got up to the piece, I examined it and thought, "Okay, still a scarf nailed to the wall." However, I began to notice the edges looked frayed and as I leaned in closer I was captivated.

I learned that what I thought was a random scarf was actually made up of twelve thousand incredibly thin needles pushed through a sheer piece of handwoven silk. I also learned that there is a point at which you can examine a piece of artwork so closely that security gets uncomfortable. But it was just so cool, and the source of inspiration for this art was also incredibly beautiful.

You see, the artist had spent time with mothers in Chicago who had lost their children to gun violence. The needles were a representation of the pain these women will endure forever, but at the same time these women are strong and beautiful, as was this piece of art.

This artist went to these hurting women whose pain has been largely ignored by the world and listened. Do you know how powerful it is for just one person to listen to your story with empathy?

It was out of compassion and a desire to share these stories that the artist felt led to create something beautiful that said, "I hear you, you matter, and your story is important." Though it may feel subtle, that's empathy, and it's the little things like this that can change our world.

* * *

One of the main reasons I take teams of people to the Syrian border is because we Westerners have the privilege of living in a bubble where we can choose not to see the hurt of the world. Our hearts are harder than we think, and they sometimes need to be wrecked in the most amazing way possible, to suffer with the other, feeling their pain as Jesus did.

Every time I go overseas, there is one night where I am overwhelmed with emotion, empathy, compassion, and—if we are being real—anger. Without fail, I spend one night of the trip secretly locked in my room with mascara running down my face, straight up ugly crying for hours. I hate it, but I know it is really good for my heart to completely shatter every once in a while. My heart needs to be broken and humbled by the kindness and radical generosity of these beautiful Syrians who have lost everything, have nothing, yet choose to love and welcome me—a complete stranger—with open arms. It keeps me grounded.

In the world of the West, it's not hard to get caught up in ourselves. It's easy to lose sight of deep empathy because it is often a choice for those of us with immense privilege. It's easy to shut down the harder emotions that come with empathy so that we don't have to suffer. In my day-to-day life, I have realized that in my advocacy work and attempts to fight injustice in our world, I can easily run on anger and push those other emotions—the ones that hurt more deeply—aside.

After the Parkland, Florida, school shooting in February 2018, my emotions were stuck in an anger that almost felt hopeless. More kids were slain inside their classrooms, more teachers lost their lives trying to shield children from bullets, another white guy became a mass murderer, and we continue to be the only developed nation where this happens on a regular basis yet we refuse to do anything about it.

A day after the shooting, my husband went into a local gun store near our children's school and tried to buy an AR-15 to learn how accessible they are. He found out that in our state you don't need a license to buy this weapon designed specifically for killing as many people as quickly as you possibly can. You do need a license for a handgun, but not an AR. In Iowa, you can walk into a gun shop and, as long as you pass a ten-minute background check, you can walk out with an AR-15. You can even finance it if you are short on cash.

It's ridiculous the lack of restrictions on these weapons, and if you want White-Jesus Christian America to get really mad at you and throw out some death threats, just make a video criticizing lax gun laws—laws that every other developed nation has implemented, with the result of no more mass shootings. Honestly, I am still pissed. I will never not be raging angry that we are willing to sacrifice our children's lives for our ability to easily purchase mass killing machines. Y'all, we should be angry. We have every right to be outraged beyond belief.

Anger has some positive effects. It fuels me to speak bolder. It fuels me to do more. But it also overwhelms my emotions, putting me into a fast-paced, problem-solving mode that allows me to bypass the feeling of hurt that comes with being wired for empathy. Without that deeper empathy, when we are solely full of an angry thirst for justice, we are slowly draining our own souls. We will eventually fade into bitter cynicism.

Months ago, someone whom I deeply admire sent my husband and me an email with some thought-provoking questions, one of which was, "When was the last time you cried for the hurting?"

At first I thought, my life revolves around seeking justice for the hurting.

But when was the last time I cried for the hurting? When was the last time I was filled with more than anger because of the hurt I saw? When was the last time I allowed myself to slow down and hurt with the hurting? Was it the last time I was on the Syrian border? At the time, that was months ago. I didn't know for sure; I couldn't think of the last time I literally cried for the hurting. And for the sake of my own heart, I realized that was a problem.

Allowing ourselves to suffer with others, to cry when the world enables needless hurt, to listen to "the other" and allow our heart to shatter—is red-letter compassion. Red-letter love entails the ultimate badass, love-seeker Jesus crying for the hurting and then doing something about it. It means allowing ourselves to hurt over and over again. It's in this place of empathy where we can truly love boldly.

Don't get me wrong. There is still a decent level of anger, and there should be. However, we have to also embrace the underlying pain that we are fighting against to truly be able to try and do this love-others stuff. We need more than just an anger for injustice. We need to slow down and feel the pain through empathy to the best of our ability. We need to cry like a small child sometimes to remind us of how real this hurt we are fighting against truly is. The pain is real, and we need to be vulnerable to that fact, because J was.

As much as I want to pretend that I'm so super tough, the reality is that's a bunch of crap. I need to cry for the hurting. We need to allow ourselves to feel. We need to embrace the pain of this world because it makes us better people. Though it may feel easier to allow anger to mask empathy, it will burn you the hell out. But a love based on compassion—even with *some* anger—is what can change this world forever. It will empower your soul and will give you life to keep fighting for love.

The way of Jesus is not to check out of emotion, it is not to ignore the hurt in our world, and it's not just being pissed at the white-washed tombs. The way of Jesus is embracing compassion, suffering with the other, and allowing ourselves to feel deeply and fight injustice with true red-letter love.

Chapter 7

SPEAK LOUDLY

Silence Is Complicity

Somewhere around the first day or so of sixth grade, I became incredibly shy—to the point that if an eighth grader would speak to me, I couldn't respond with more than two words while inwardly I had a massive anxiety attack. My insane social anxiety faded by the time I got to high school, but still, unless I was high or drunk, I generally was the girl in conversation who sat back and listened, rarely contributing a word.

Even though I could hear and technically I could talk, I'm still reminded of myself when I imagine the time Jesus healed a deaf and mute guy by putting his spit on the man's tongue, and suddenly the man could speak and hear like a boss (Mark 7:33–35). I bet that guy spoke loudly when he found his voice. No one spit on me that I know of, but when I finally did find my voice, I had the tendency to become fiery as hell when it came to certain topics of conversation.

Do you know what ended up being the equivalent of spit on my tongue? Social justice. Though I still could and can be somewhat shy, I found when I was passionate about something, I would generally speak out boldly, no problem.

As we talked about way back in the first section of this book, in my early twenties, I was your basic fiery, and honestly, kind of angry liberal-type. My passion wasn't about trying to follow the ways of Jesus per se; my passion was rooted in the desire to see justice for the hurting. My agenda wasn't necessarily to love others; it was to fight for them or with them or just fight in general, if we are being honest.

When I started trying to follow the ways of Jesus, something slowly shifted. I was still fiery and passionate, but my desire became to love, not fight.

Now you may be thinking, "Well, Sheri, it seems like you are pretty pissed with White-Jesus Christians; it looks more like you want to fight on that front." That's a valid thought; my husband says I yell in my writing. However, there is far more to it these days.

We tend to think of Jesus as passive, as if love is merely a feeling, not an action. But Jesus had some serious passion and wasn't afraid to put himself in the middle of tension and speak out against those who he saw causing the most hurt.

Think about how Jesus spoke out against the religious elite of his day. He spoke out boldly and broadly, publically spoke out and criticized this group using a broad brush—and he could be harsh. Real talk. Speaking out is a major part of resisting. It's an important action that Jesus took, and we need to as well.

So let's talk about Jesus #nofilter.

"Then Jesus said to the crowds and to his disciples, 'The scribes and the Pharisees sit on Moses' seat; therefore, do whatever they teach you and follow it; but do not do as they do, for they do not practice what they teach'" (Matt. 23:1–3).

Jesus isn't calling someone out one-on-one here. This is a public roast session, y'all.

"They tie up heavy burdens, hard to bear, and lay them on the shoulders of others; but they themselves are unwilling to lift a finger to move them. They do all their deeds to be seen by others; for they make their phylacteries broad and their fringes long. They love to have the place of honor at banquets and the best seats in the synagogues, and to be greeted with respect in the marketplaces, and to have people call them rabbi. But you are not to be called rabbi, for you have one teacher, and you are all students. And call no one your father on earth, for you have one Father—the one in heaven. Nor are you to be called instructors, for you have one instructor, the Messiah. The greatest among you will be your servant. All who exalt themselves will be humbled, and all who humble themselves will be exalted.

"But woe to you, scribes and Pharisees, hypocrites! For you lock people out of the kingdom of heaven. For you do not go in yourselves, and when others are going in, you stop them. Woe to you, scribes and Pharisees, hypocrites! For you cross sea and land to make a single convert, and you make the new convert twice as much a child of hell as yourselves."

Matt. 23:4–15

Jesus goes on and on, slamming the religious with enthusiasm saying, "woe to you, scribes and Pharisees, hypocrites!" five more times! He calls them a "brood of vipers," and "white-washed tombs," calling out their greed and injustice, their external show of holiness, while masking the rot in their souls. Clean on the outside but gross and dirty within.

What do you think his motive was in calling out the religious elite? As harsh as he sounded, I bet his motive was not to fight with the scribes and Pharisees. Jesus spoke out boldly against those claiming to follow the guy he called God the Father, but in reality, we're using the name of G-O-D while hurting others. Jesus' motive was to love those who were being hurt—point blank.

Here's the thing: if we don't speak out against the religious elite of our own day, if we stay silent as I did as an awkward tween, nothing will change in this world. Without our voice we cannot be the change we want to see. And to be honest, a life of silence sucks.

In his "Letter from Birmingham Jail," Dr. Martin Luther King Jr., one of the most amazing peacemakers, and who I think most of us would agree boldly followed the ways of Jesus, wrote, "We will have to repent in this generation not merely for the hateful words and actions of bad people but for the appalling silence of good people." I believe he's as on point today as he was then.

Your voice is important, and your voice is needed. Your silence doesn't keep peace; it enables hurt. It is your voice that will let love win.

* * *

I want to tell you about one of my biggest failures, a failure that burned the MLK quote above into my brain forever.

I cannot say I know when this failure—my silence, my ignorance—began; what I can say is that it was at its height when I was teaching during the 2015–16 school year, when the presidential primaries were hot and contro-versial. I was teaching history at an alternative high school in an urban area of Houston, and the demographic of my amazing students were for the most part Latina and Latino, many of whom where Dreamers—immigrants who had been brought to the U.S. as children.

During the first week of our U.S. History class we discussed America's first national motto, *E Pluribus Unum*, which means "Out of Many, One," and we all agreed that one cool attribute of America is the many immigrants and diverse cultures that make up this nation.

Throughout the year, many of my students shared with me their own stories of crossing the southern border, coming to the U.S. with their families in search of a better life. They shared experiences of the violence they had fled and the horrible things some of them had seen as children that would rival even ISIS in its level of atrociousness.

Quite a few of my kids' parents were not able to make parent-teacher conferences because they worked multiple jobs in order to support their family. But whenever I called these parents, they all spoke of their deep desire for their children to do well and make a better life for themselves. It was crystal clear how proud they were of their kids and how every sacrifice they made to come to this country was out of love.

These amazing people are an asset; they make America great.

As the 2015–16 school year began and the election season heated up with campaign promises of mass deportation and a giant border wall between the U.S. and Mexico, naturally, many of my students voiced some concern for their families. And I responded with every bit of assurance as I told them the chances of this candidate being elected and carrying out these super-racist policies was pretty much nonexistent. There was no way, right?

Through the year we talked about emancipation, the progressive era, the women's suffrage movement, the civil rights movement—countless fights for equality all throughout this nation's history. We discussed historical voices and movements of resistance against oppression and how important it is that we practice our rights and vocally stand against intolerance. We talked about the Chinese Exclusion Act and Executive Order 9066 and my kids asked if this was Trump's goal. Again, with every bit of confidence, I said that regardless of the very real problem of racism in our country, a government policy so blatantly and outwardly prejudiced would not happen today. That executive order went against the constitution; I couldn't imagine a replay of this sort of broad intolerance coming from the executive branch of the U.S. government. I mean, the people wouldn't have it, right?

By the end of the school year, the voices calling for a wall and deportation were growing stronger as Trump won primary after primary, and my students understandably still questioned their future and expressed a valid fear of watching the unimaginable history we'd learned about repeat itself. Maybe I was in a state of denial—I seriously could not fathom the reality that was coming to fruition—so I continued to reassure them that they and their families would be safe.

But I was wrong. I lied to them.

As the next school year began, we watched the election unfold and this new administration begin to cash in on its promises directly aimed at hurting the families of my students, policies I assured them couldn't happen. My heart broke. I was dead wrong. I dismissed their concerns with my comforting words, that when is all said and done, were lies.

You see, I taught expansively through history the vitality of resisting oppression, yet I stood in denial for far too long thinking this could never happen again, not here, not today. Until it did, and we failed. I failed. A "leader" elected largely for his hateful immigration/ refugee policy took power and tried to carry out the detestable policies that I told my students wouldn't happen. You see, being a white person with an American passport, I had the privilege of standing in denial through the escalation until everything erupted. However, I stood in denial at the expense of others being hurt.

I am sharing this because it is a massive failure. I should not have waited to boldly speak out; I should have listened to my students' concerns and instead of simply offering comforting words, I should have—we all should have—gone to the streets to loudly speak out before their fears could become reality. I am sharing this in hopes that we learn to listen better, love bolder, and speak out against the hurt we see today.

Our voices matter. What if we all would have spoken out against the outrageous policies that were largely supported by White-Jesus Christians then? The ways of Jesus are not passive. Love is not passive: love is standing in the middle of the tension and speaking out. It's marching in solidarity against oppression like we did in the Women's March and the March for Our Lives. It's standing firm against the hurt in our world like we see in the Black Lives Matter movement, the airport protests against the Muslim ban and deportation of immigrants, and the #MeToo movement. It's calling out the "white-washed" tombs in our own society regardless of the backlash we will receive. It's loudly practicing nonviolent resistance like Martin Luther King Jr did. It's choosing to use privilege to get over ourselves and give a voice to the marginalized, just like Jesus did a couple thousand years ago.

What if we questioned what our pastor or religion or YouTube idol tells us that we are supposed to believe about major societal issues and look at what the words of Jesus tell us?

In the second section of this book, I hope that we can do just that. Simply consider the contrast between the world and the red letters when it comes to issues like racism, violence, nationalism, misogyny, and more. Again, my hope is not to change you to fit my views; my hope is that this book provokes you to look a little deeper into basically the meaning of anything and everything through the red letters. Re-examine what you thought you knew in a different light and come to your own conclusions, not your pastor's, not your parents', not mine—your own beliefs. Beliefs that, if filtered through the ways of Jesus, are formed on a foundation of love. Because let's be real, we need to let love win in our world.

PART II
RED-LETTERED GLASSES

Chapter 8

CAN WE STAND
IN THE MIDDLE?

Racism

Never in my life did I think I would see hundreds of actual, self-proclaimed Nazis and KKK members marching on the streets of the U.S., carrying tiki torches and assault rifles, yelling "Blood and Soil" and then watch people, White-Jesus Christians in particular, defend or refuse to condemn the actions of these hateful racists. But really, I also never thought in a billion years that Trump could win an election that allowed him to become the leader of this lovely nation. So, really, what do I know? I mean, at this point, we basically live in the regressive era of America.

For years we have seen multiple murders and police brutality toward unarmed people of color caught on video, even live-streamed on Facebook, yet we still act as if the reality of deep racism in this nation is up for debate. I mean, do you know how many of these officers have been convicted of first-degree murder? Well, as of 2017, the answer is zero. Hopefully by the time you read these words that stat has changed. It's as if we are allowing officers to legally kill people of color and then arguing that there isn't a problem with racism.

The police brutality we see toward people of color is no better today than it was in the midst of the civil rights movement. And during that era, where did we see much of the White American Church? Many were heading coalitions of racists using the name of White-Jesus as they used any tactic they could think of to dehumanize and even physically harm peaceful protesters whose goals were something that White-Jesus clearly wants no part in— equality.

Then there were the White Christian moderates, those who believed in equality and inwardly were opposed to racism but didn't join the resistance. They stayed out of the tension and sat on the sideline quietly rooting for equality of all. In his "Letter from Birmingham Jail," Dr. Martin Luther King Jr had some pretty direct words for these types.

> First, I must confess that over the last few years I have been gravely disappointed with the white moderate. I have almost reached the regrettable conclusion that the Negro's great stumbling block in the stride toward freedom is not the White Citizen's Council-er or the Ku Klux Klanner, but the white moderate who is more devoted to "order" than to justice; who prefers a negative peace which is the absence of tension to a positive peace which is the presence of justice; who constantly says "I agree with you in the goal you seek, but I can't agree with your methods of direct action."[1]

Dr. King straight up stated that the greatest barrier to freedom was the white moderate. And this is what we still see within much of white Christianity today. We see those condemning movements against racism like the Black Lives Matter Movement while supporting the "rights" of white supremacists to express their hateful ideology and deploy their scare tactics. And we still have those white moderates who try to stay out of the conflict, thinking that by not getting involved and speaking out directly, they are being "peacemakers."

Y'all, the American Church has deep roots in white supremacy and racism, from manifest destiny, to slavery, to fighting the civil rights movement, to blatant white privilege, to allowing police brutality while negating the sufferings of our brothers and sisters of color. We know this. But what I can't understand even more than the ignorant racists are the false allies who try to play the middle ground as if that would be the way of Jesus.

Let me give you an example of what I mean. The day after a white supremacist drove his car into a crowd of antiracist counter-protesters at a white Nazi—I mean white "nationalist"—rally you would think the church would speak out strongly from their Sunday morning platform. Not only did our commander-in-tweet refuse to condemn this I-don't-know-how-it-could-be-more-straight-up racism, but a bunch of White-Jesus mega pastors with a ton of influence did the same. In fact, the pulpit of most (though not all) white pastors was silent. While many may have felt they were against racism, they chose not to publically condemn or even acknowledge the extreme hate that surrounds us. Why is that?

The truth of the matter is twofold.

Though most churches aren't straight up calling for KKK rallies, too many white Christians still hold a sense of racial superiority. We see it in the constant white Christian resistance to Black Lives Matter, in the hashtag #notallwhitepeople, and in the denial of white privilege. When we ignorantly deny the existence of systemic racism in our nation, we ourselves are the problem.

Secondly, there are bs church politics. The reason that probably the majority of white Christian pastors are claiming "middle ground" and not speaking out against racism during this time is because they want to stay out of the drama, and really try super hard not to piss off any big tithers. A lot of white Christians just want that feel-good Sunday morning experience and truly believe in staying out of the tension of social issues so as to not make enemies.

So the real question is, what would Jesus do? Would he have stayed neutral? Would he have just stayed out of it? Would he have viewed pursuing peace as staying out of the tension and not making his own people uncomfortable?

I doubt it.

These questions remind me of the time Jesus walked into a synagogue on the day of Sabbath. (I promise this isn't a bad joke.) The law of Moses has all these rules about the Sabbath, like you can't work or cure people or take too many steps, you know, normal religious-like stuff.

So in the synagogue was a man with a super messed up hand; "withered," they called it. Jesus had been healing people all over the place, but—oh wait—he wasn't supposed to do that on the Sabbath. So the religious elite are standing around just waiting for Jesus to screw up and break the dumb rules in front of everybody, in the actual synagogue.

So what did J do?

"Come over here," he said to the man, and scanning the room, he posed a question: "Is it lawful to do good or to do harm on the sabbath, to save life or to kill?" (Mark 3:4).

Then came the awkward silence; everyone just stood around feeling super uncomfortable. Jesus looked around and got a little angry but also sad because all of these guys were being jerks and acting as if their hearts were made of stone.

So Jesus said, "All right dude, stretch out your hand." And the guy with the withered hand stretches his hand out and—no joke—it was healed, looking again like a totally normal hand.

So the religious elite then got super pissed and went to conspire to kill Jesus because they have some serious anger issues. (See Mark 3:1–6 for the details.)

The "proper" thing to do would have been for Jesus to stay quiet and not upset all the religious folk. Jesus could have easily just chilled, healed the guy in private, or waited until the next day. But the thing is, saying nothing would have been wrong, waiting until Sabbath to be over to heal the guy to avoid tension would have been wrong.

What did Jesus truly care about? He didn't care in the least about what his fellow Jews thought of him; he cared about loving the hurt. He didn't stay silent; he spoke out to the whole room of cold-hearted uppity religious. He didn't take the safe path to not upset anyone; he took a side and spoke out with those who were hurting.

* * *

The thing with taking the middle ground is that it almost feels rational because people get seriously mad if you speak out—it makes them uncomfortable. (Trust me, I know.) We think that if we speak out boldly against the actions and ideology of the other side, they (the other side) probably won't listen to our words. But maybe if we stay in the middle, we can have a conversation and try to slowly change the oppressor's views. We could win them over first, and then address the deep issues that our nation faces. I absolutely believe that we should always be willing to listen and converse with whoever the other is. And yes, it is a ton easier to have a conversation with someone who holds contradicting views if they aren't already pissed that we boldly speak out against their ideology or the ideology of a people group they relate to. Makes sense, right?

Imagine a group of ten teenage girls. (If you didn't immediately picture the cast of *Mean Girls*, do so now.) Four of the girls have super wealthy parents and life is pretty lavish. They feel that they own the world because they are basically Regina George (queen bee of the afore-mentioned movie). Four of the girls are your average high schoolers; they play soccer and take yearbook photos and are generally just pretty chill—kind of like Lindsay Lohan before she joined "the plastics"—aka the club of rich, mean girls. The other two girls are the head of the math club; they are super nice and smart but stand out with their brightly colored "mathlete" jackets.

The four Regina Georges start being super mean to the two mathlete girls. They make super discriminatory jokes, they send mean snapchats of the girls to the entire school, and they shove them into lockers while calling them losers. Some of that really mean, unwarranted stuff teenage girls can do. The mathlete girls are for sure the minority, and they are completely unsuccessful in their attempts to stop the four Regina George plastics from being complete jerks.

So the four average, chill girls notice this happening and think it's totally messed up, because it is. They've per-sonally never had a problem with either the Regina George plastics or the mathlete girls.

Two of the chill girls don't directly intervene but stay more neutral, and they are able to have some subtle conver-sation with the Regina George plastics. And guess what? The Regina Georges actually let them explain their view because they are doing so in a nonthreatening manner. So they are able to keep a conversation open by not directly calling the mean girls out. Smart, right?

The other two chill girls take a different route. They say, screw this, and call out the mean girls' treatment of the mathlete girls. Even though they were originally cool with both sides, they took a clear side with the girls who were hurting and became vocal in the school about the discrimination they were seeing. They start speaking to other students organizing meetings, getting the administration involved, and even holding protests with the mathlete girls fighting together against the bullying ideology of the Regina George mean girls.

Now, do you think that any of the Regina George types would have a conversation with the protesters or listen to anything they said after they had blatantly and harshly called them out? No, probably not.

But here is the thing. How long, if ever, would it take for the girls who took the middle ground to neutrally talk the Regina Georges out of being jerks? And while we are waiting for subtle conversations of persuasion, who is continuing to suffer? It's not the chill girls; they come from a place a privilege, a place in which they are not directly suffering. They have the choice to stay passive and neutral or stand with the oppressed, but what they choose is at the expense of those who are being hurt.

You see, if no one calls out the oppression, it won't change. If no one stands up directly against racism, racists win. Yeah, we may be able to have less-heated conversations with them and try to convince them to change their views, but this conversation would be long and drawn out and it would be at the expense of our brothers and sisters of color who are suffering daily. It's because of our privilege that we can choose to stay neutral while others are being hurt.

Martin Luther King Jr. said, "In the end, we will not remember the words of our enemies, but the silence of our friends." What was his stance on vocally opposing oppression, and why do we think that playing the middle ground would produce any different result than it did then? It may not be comfortable to stand in the middle of tension, but to be on the side of the oppressed you either stand with them in the tension or you fail to love them for the sake of personal false peace.

Personally, I would rather be criticized and even hated for my voice than to sit silently in the middle during this regressive era of racism and oppression. It's hard for me to believe that the way of Jesus would be to stay passive and neutral while others are hurting.

Think about the life of Jesus. Were there any groups of people Jesus focused more of his attention on? To say no to this question would be completely inaccurate. Jesus straight up spent his time going out of his way to love and hang out with those on the fringe, those who faced injustice. Jesus hung out with the lepers, the prostitutes, *women* (gasp!), Samaritans, the sick, the poor, the hurting, the Gentiles. Jesus sought out the marginalized and extended bold love—that was just the way he was.

Did all lives matter to Jesus? Yes, for sure. But Jesus stood strongly with those who faced injustice. He didn't play the middle ground between the religious elite and those who were facing discrimination. He always stood for and with the hurting, and he continuously and broadly called out the oppressive religious elite for their treatment of others. Jesus publicly called the religious elite "broods

of vipers," and he didn't even say #NotAllPharisees, even though I bet not all Pharisees were complete jerks.

Why would we ever think that J would play the middle ground? Looking at his life, why would we doubt for a second that Jesus would be standing firm with people of color while calling out neo-Nazis, the presidents and pastors who defend them, and every aspect of systemic racism that we continually see poisoning our society? If Jesus stands with the oppressed, shouldn't those who are trying to follow his ways be standing on that side as well? The question now is, which side is "Christian America" standing on and which side will we choose? Y'all, we would never see Jesus on the sidelines, wanting to end racism but too afraid of conflict with the oppressors. Jesus would be marching with our brothers and sisters of color because his way is never silence; his way is the way of always boldly loving others.

Chapter 9

UNEXCEPTIONAL EXCEPTIONALISM

Nationalism

If I told you I don't say the pledge of allegiance, and that I didn't say it even when I was a teacher and it ran every day during announcements, what would you think? Be truthful, would it make you as angry as those red Starbucks cups did in 2016?

Really, I'm sure some of y'all would think that I am a freedom-hating communist. I'm not; I don't hate freedom. I am grateful to live in a country where I have had immense and completely undeserved privilege, a nation in which I have the freedom to personally choose not to pledge to a nation-state. Truly, I am not anti-America in the slightest. However, I am not on board with the state of nationalism in this country; to be honest, it's a bit cult-like.

During the 2016 election, we heard the voice of nationalism on steroids as the idea of "America First" constantly rang loudly in our ears like the hook of a bad Taylor Swift song.

When you mix this extreme nationalism with a religion, Christianity, you get a hot White-Jesus, America-first mess. Seeing that Jesus stands on the side of the poor and oppressed, not the rich and powerful, the ways of Jesus are pretty hard to align with an ideology that sees America as our God-given promised land (well, after we wiped out the natives in the name of Jesus), America as the blessed

Christian nation of a God who definitely likes white Americans more than pretty much everyone else, and plain-old America First. This idea of America as a "city on a hill" dates back to 1630, when John Winthrop envisioned the Puritan colony as a light to the nations. And maybe we are a light on a hill—a light that ends up starting a forest fire that destroys the rest of the world. When we see a church choir sing a "Make America Great Again" song, proclaiming Donald Trump's signature slogan as an act of worship, we have passed into the realm of a nationalistic cult obsession. It's kind of like the eerie flashbacks from a post-apocalyptic movie—that vibe like it's not the end of the world yet, but it's definitely coming.

Americans' desire for (reclaimed?) greatness isn't unique. Jesus' contemporaries wanted to make Israel great again. I mean, the struggle was real: Israel was under Roman occupation, made to pay taxes to an empire they despised and tiptoe around foreign soldiers posted in their towns.

People in Jesus' day thought the point of the messiah they were waiting for was to restore greatness to the nation of Israel, and they were super confused when Jesus came constantly talking about things like bringing the kingdom and destroying the temple as he hung out with the weirdos that many people would never be caught chilling with.

Jesus actually didn't really talk about the political situation his people were in; it just wasn't his thing. The story that comes to mind as far as Jesus and "the man" goes would be the time when the Pharisees sent their peeps and some Herodians to try and publically trip Jesus up with a question. You see, the Pharisees were wildly nationalistic and hated Jesus because he called them out on their egocentrism and hypocrisy. The Herodians came together when the Romans appointed Herod as the regional puppet king who got some nice perks from the Romans in return for their cooperation. The Herodians also weren't fans of Jesus because they were nervous he would ignite a revolution that would lead to the Romans stripping away their power.

So they came to Jesus in an attempt to catch him slipping up in his words, and I would imagine the conversation went something like the following: "So here is the deal, we are a fan. We can see that you speak about God in truth and no one can persuade you away from your truth because you really don't care about the haters, which is awesome. So the thing is, we are curious; do you think we should pay taxes to Caesar, that guy who oppresses our nation, or not so much?"

Jesus knew they were trying to get him to slip up, so he responded with, "Y'all are total hypocrites, why are you trying to trap me in my words? Bring me the coin used for paying this tax."

So they brought him a denarius—which I think is a cool word but that is totally irrelevant—and Jesus asked, "Okay, so who is this guy on here?"

"Um, well, it's Caesar," they replied, probably a bit nervous as to where Jesus was going with this.

"So give to Caesar what is Caesar's and give to God what is God's," Jesus said.

And the people were like, "Damn, this guy knows what's up." (See Matt. 22:15–22 for details.)

You see, the reason his answer was so on point is twofold. Basically, Jesus sounded like a super sarcastic badass, or at least that's how I imagine it. If he would have straight up said, "Yes, pay taxes to Caesar—you know, the guy who makes us suffer," the regular folk Jesus hung around with would probably get super pissed. I mean they thought they were waiting for someone to make Israel great again, not support the evil empire.

If J went the opposite direction and said, "No, don't pay the taxes to that d-bag," he may have been arrested on the spot by the Herodians out of that fear that he was igniting an uprising. Typical Heriodians, always looking out for their own self-interest over the freedom of their people.

This is basically the only time Jesus addressed political issues, and he did not give an answer that pleased the Jewish nationalists or the supporters of the Empire. He kind of said to pay your taxes, but in a way that felt like more of a smart-ass, money-has-no-real-meaning type of jab. Not quite what people were hoping. Too bad; "Make Israel Great Again" (MIGA) would have made an excellent platform for Jesus.

* * *

Though Jesus didn't talk much about politics, his teachings have a lot to do with the issues that fill our political realm today. And since people wrongly thought Jesus was going to MIGA, let's look more at those assumptions and Jesus' response. There is a story about Jesus that explains this quite spot on.

When he [Jesus] came to Nazareth, where he had been brought up, he went to the synagogue on the sabbath day, as was his custom. He stood up to read, and the scroll of the prophet Isaiah was given to him. He unrolled the scroll and found the place where it was written:
"The Spirit of the Lord is upon me, because he has anointed me to bring good news to the poor. He

has sent me to proclaim release to the captives and recovery of sight to the blind, to let the oppressed go free, to proclaim the year of the Lord's favor."

And he rolled up the scroll, gave it back to the attendant, and sat down. The eyes of all in the synagogue were fixed on him. Then he began to say to them, "Today this scripture has been fulfilled in your hearing."

All spoke well of him and were amazed at the gracious words that came from his mouth. They said, "Is not this Joseph's son?"

Luke 4:16–22

The people were super excited because they thought he was saying he was there to make Israel great again, freeing the oppressed and proclaiming the year of the Lord's favor, just as the prophet foretold! Israel was coming back, baby. Yay MIGA!

And then this happened.

He said to them, "Doubtless you will quote to me this proverb, 'Doctor, cure yourself!' And you will say, 'Do here also in your hometown the things that we have heard you did at Capernaum.'"

And he said, "Truly I tell you, no prophet is accepted in the prophet's hometown. But the truth is, there were many widows in Israel in the time of Elijah, when the heaven was shut up three years and six months, and there was a severe famine over all the land; yet Elijah was sent to none of them except to a widow at Zarephath in Sidon. There were also many lepers in Israel in the time of the prophet Elisha, and none of them was cleansed except Naaman the Syrian." When they heard this, all in the synagogue were filled with rage. They got up, drove him out of the town, and led him to the brow of the hill on which their town was built, so that they might hurl him off the cliff. But he passed through the midst of them and went on his way.

Luke 4:23–30

So now the same people who were like, "Yay, this guy is cool" just two minutes ago, want to throw him off a cliff. Talk about some drastic mood swings.

So how did Jesus manage to piss off the super nationalistic people of Israel here?

Basically, he inferred that like Elijah saved the foreign widow and Elisha healed the Syrian, he was not there to free the long-oppressed nation of Israel from the Roman Empire, but he was there to heal and bring some of that love to the most marginalized of the world—widows, lepers, and foreigners.

They were supposed to be God's favorite! Freedom wasn't supposed to be given to others! If the Messiah was not simply there to MIGA, but to offer a crazy bold love to all, including even communists and Muslims, then Israel was not first in the eyes of God. They actually were not superior to the rest of the world like a certain country seems to think they are today.

With Jesus, it was never about nationalism. It was always about an inclusive love for all, a sacrificial love toward the most vulnerable in society. Maybe there is something we can learn here, America—from Jesus, and from history.

* * *

There once was a nation . . . let's call it Germany. In World War I, Germany had fought with and against many other nations and, unfortunately for them, landed on the losing side. Though other nations lost the war as well, Germany was punished more severely than any other, and its economy was destroyed with little hope in sight.

Decades later, the world was in the midst of the Great Depression and Germany was still hurting. The people of Germany were pissed. They felt they had been treated far too harshly after the war. They were sick of struggling. Thus began a movement, and a party arose called the National Socialist German Workers' Party, aka Nazis.

The Nazis desperately wanted to make Germany great again. They were radically nationalistic and were able to come together under their shared passion for their nation—that is, the "Real Germans" of their nation. The Nazis despised anyone who didn't fit their definition of a "pure" Germany: gypsies, Jehovah's witnesses, gay people, and especially Jews. The Jewish people had managed to stay wealthy throughout these hard times while others of Germany struggled severely, which really annoyed people.

So the Nazis grew and grew in its radical nationalism, all while calling themselves positive Christians, until one day they became the ruling party of the nation of Germany, under their super charismatic leader, Adolf Hitler, who was really good at public speaking and eventually was able to turn the country into a totalitarian state, but in the "positive Christian" sort of way. Sounds pretty sketch, but hey, the people just wanted their nation to be great again.

So the Nazis started expanding their power, even taking over neighboring nations. I mean, why not spread their ways of greatness through the world, right? They also rounded up all these people they thought were inferior to the white, positive Christian people of Germany, and put them in containment camps, breaking families apart, using them as slave labor, starving them in the process, and ultimately locking them in a room and murdering them with poison gas, then burning their bodies in human ovens—mass genocide in some of the most horrific manners imaginable. The Nazis ended up murdering over six million Jewish people. It's just what they ultimately had to do to make Germany great again.

I wish I could say this story is one of dark fiction, but as we both know, it's not. The point to this story is that none of this would have happened without a deep sense of nationalistic pride, a desire to make their nation great again, and some fabricated religious statements that tied it all together and baptized it in the name of Christ. Germany was struggling, so the voice that preached unifying in greatness was appealing, and it was surely what God wanted. That is until things got out of hand, and millions of people were slaughtered.

I bring this up to say, nationalism can be hella dangerous. It only takes a few steps to transform from hard core country-loving nationalists into the realm of fascism. Don't get me wrong, I am not saying you shouldn't love your country. Patriotism is cool. Patriotism says, "I really like and am proud of where I come from," and that is great. Nationalism, on the other hand, says we are better than everybody else and we deserve more, regardless of who we destroy in the process. When paired with Christianity, nationalism can claim that God is on board with our exceptional deservingness, so whatever we need to do to be great is cool—I mean, we are a self-proclaimed Christian nation, right? But so was Nazi Germany.

If Christians buy into this America First mentality, we are essentially saying that God loves people more or less based on the nationality on their passports, like Israel did in Jesus' day and again but much differently like Nazi Germany did during World War II. Do we really think the lives of our children are more important to God than the lives of non-American children? Do we think we deserve greatness just because we claim the name of Christianity? White-Jesus nationalism is basically the prosperity gospel on crack.

So let's ask ourselves this: How would Jesus want us to respond to the intense nationalism we see today as well as how we interact with and love others first? What if instead of MIGA or MAGA, we focused on making the ways of Jesus' red-letter love great again? Jesus came to free the hearts of the people, many of whom were so obsessed with making Israel great again that they completely missed what truly mattered. In the culture of America First White-Jesus Christianity, we also may be missing the entire point—to love others first. All others—not just fellow white Christian Americans.

Chapter 10
BAN THE WALLS
Refuge

If our world was a high school cafeteria, the U.S. would be the table of cool kids who think they are awesome but really are just mean and exclusive, and most of the other nation-tables can't stand them but for some reason they hold the power in the school. And let's face it, when we have watched a nation's "leader" flip out on Twitter because another nation's leader called him old, it's pretty much on the same level of bs drama as high school, only much more dangerous because there are nuclear weapons involved.

Both within our nation and around the world, we tend to be pretty discriminatory about who we are willing to sit with or welcome into society. And rather than the church being that one kid who is comfortable enough in her own skin to stand outside the popularity contest and befriend everybody, it tends to be the worst offender. White-Jesus Christianity is basically the Regina George of our world.

The inclusive nature of Jesus compared with the exclusiveness of White-Jesus Christians is a tragic indictment of our faith. As the U.S. shuts out, kicks out, and denies equality to many groups of people, how does our response and rationale align with the ways of Jesus?

Toward the end of his time on earth, Jesus made a statement, as he often did, that would cause some controversy that has lasted thousands, yes, thousands of years. What was it this time? Well, he said the following:

"When the Son of Man comes in his glory, and all the angels with him, then he will sit on the throne of his glory. All the nations will be gathered before him, and he will separate people one from another as a shepherd separates the sheep from the goats, and he will put the sheep at his right hand and the goats at the left.

Then the king will say to those at his right hand, 'Come, you that are blessed by my Father, inherit the kingdom prepared for you from the foundation of the world; for I was hungry and you gave me food, I was thirsty and you gave me something to drink, I was a stranger and you welcomed me, I was naked and you gave me clothing, I was sick and you took care of me, I was in prison and you visited me.'

"Then the righteous will answer him, 'Lord, when was it that we saw you hungry and gave you food, or thirsty and gave you something to drink? And when was it that we saw you a stranger and welcomed you, or naked and gave you clothing? And when was it that we saw you sick or in prison and visited you?'

"And the king will answer them, 'Truly I tell you, just as you did it to one of the least of these who are members of my family, you did it to me.'

"Then he will say to those at his left hand, . . for I was hungry and you gave me no food, I was thirsty and you gave me nothing to drink, I was a stranger and you did not welcome me, naked and you did not give me clothing, sick and in prison and you did not visit me.'

"Then they also will answer, 'Lord, when was it that we saw you hungry or thirsty or a stranger or naked or sick or in prison, and did not take care of you?' Then he will answer them, 'Truly I tell you, just as you did not do it to one of the least of these, you did not do it to me.'"

Matt. 25:31–45

So basically, Jesus is describing two groups of people: goat people and sheep people. Like dog people and cat people, only one is clearly superior to the other. The sheep people are compassionate and generous toward people in need and don't even realize how significant their kindness is—so significant that it's like showing kindness to Jesus himself. The goat people, on the other hand, ignore the needs of others and try to defend themselves, saying, "If it had been you, Jesus, we totally would have stopped to help!" Jesus responds, "No. If you ignore them, you ignore me."

Now you may be wondering why this statement would be controversial in these days, and in those days. I mean, Jesus is talking about feeding the poor, caring for the sick, clothing the naked, all super nice things, why would any of this be provocative?

Well, because too often, we don't want to do these things.

That goat life takes the hearts of many in White-Jesus Christianity, and we see a lot of backs turned on the least of these—the hurting, the vulnerable, the hungry.

We can see goats all over the spectrum, in issues like hunger, poverty, lack of access to clean water, and overflowing prisons. These are all super important, but I want to talk here about an arena that was super personal to Jesus himself: welcoming the stranger.

Back in the day, when little eight-pound, six-ounce baby Jesus was born, a king named Herod heard a rumor that the King of the Jews had arrived. So since Herod was king and apparently super paranoid, he completely lost his shit and decided to have all the little boys around Bethlehem who were under two years old murdered. Yep, that was the plan.

Luckily for J, before the mass slaughter of small children began, Joseph, Jesus' adoptive dad or stepdad, or foster dad (it's hard to know what to call him), got a tip from an angelic being that baby J was in danger and they needed to take off. So they did what anyone who feared for the life of their child would do; they got up in the middle of the night, grabbed whatever they could hold on to, and fled for their lives. In an instant, they lost everything—their home, any fragment of a life they had built, really, everything they knew. Overnight their entire world changed as they became refugees seeking safety.

Now here is the hard part. Imagine a family from the Middle East with a little baby, knocking on our red, white, and blue door in search of refuge, in search of safety for their small child. What do you think we, as a nation, would do?

"Oh, Jesus, we would totally let *you* in! A crazy king is trying to kill you!"

A crazy king? Like a leader using chemical weapons to massacre the small children of his own nation? Or a drug lord threatening to dismember your entire family if you don't let him take your young daughter and use her for sex trafficking?

We all know what our nation would do if baby refugee Jesus knocked on our door, because he has been knocking and continues to knock, while we add another deadbolt and chain lock. Our nation has passed bans prohibiting the immigration of those who are suffering just as baby Jesus and his family did. If it were today, we would literally detain Jesus in the airport and ship him back to his certain death without missing a sip of our Kombucha.

Luckily for baby J, not all nations shared the views of our nation when it comes to those seeking safety. Jesus' family was able to find refuge in Egypt for years until Herod finally died and they were able to go back to their home nation. Apparently, Egypt back in the day was far kinder than we, the U.S., are today when it comes to these sorts of matters.

This is the reality of what we see today as our nation reacts to the mass hurt of the refugee crisis we see in our world as we respond to the millions of displaced men, women, children, and tiny babies all around the world, who have lost everything.

When we saw them hungry, we stress ate our super-sized fries.

When we saw them thirsty, we kept walking, sipping our organic, vegan green smoothies.

When we saw a stranger who had lost everything, we ignored them and continued to watch the Kardashians.

When we saw them naked, we sent old, mismatched shoes.

When we saw them sick, and imprisoned, and being tortured, we turned off the news.

The ways of White-Jesus close our doors to the most vulnerable, the ways of White-Jesus do not give a second look to those who have lost everything, the ways of White-Jesus would never even look at the refugee Jesus in need.

Are we okay with this? Are we okay living in a goat nation that bans those most in need of radical welcome and bold love? If not, we have to be willing to go against the grain and live that red-letter sheep life. On the line is not only our very souls, but the lives of millions we can choose to see and love.

* * *

Can I be blunt? (More so than usual, that is?) Sometimes I get super angry about some of the horrible things we see in the world and then the response of White-Jesus Christianity. I know, you are shocked by this revelation. As we have watched refugee crises unfold for years, the domestic reaction has been one of the most troubling events that I have witnessed, in part because it is personal to my heart and in part because I like to think I am a semi-decent, non-sociopathic human.

"'Why do you call me "Lord, Lord," and do not do what I tell you?'" Jesus said (Luke 6:46).

These are the words of Jesus that ring in my ears when I am trapped in a spiral of inner tension regarding the ways of American White-Jesus Christianity. There are times when the tension breaks me and I snap, in a sense. What I am going to share with y'all right now is one of those times.

I was sitting on a rooftop near the Jordanian border of Syria in April 2017, when Syrian dictator Bashar al-Assad used chemical weapons on his own people, brutally slaughtering the innocent. Donald Trump responded by launching an airstrike at one of Assad's military bases. My soul broke, and I wrote the following letter.

Dear America,
  Self-proclaimed Christian nation, I wish the lives of others mattered to you as much as Starbucks coffee cups. I know the guy you call Savior instructed you to love others as yourselves, but that seems to have become more of a catchy phrase than an actual command to live by.
  A few days ago, a handful of miles north of where I am sitting right now, a chemical attack massacred innocent Syrian children as they slept. As the Internet floods with yet more images of small, limp, lifeless bodies piling up, my heart falls apart knowing this just adds to the atrocities the world watches yet refuses to respond to with love.
  You see, yesterday I spent the afternoon with one of the most beautiful and kind families I have ever encountered. They are refugees from Syria, and like millions of others, they have lost everything while going through the unimaginable. After fleeing their homes, everything they have ever known, they are now stranded on the border of Jordan as the majority of the world doesn't seem to care more than expressing a shallow sense of sorrow at what "those poor people" have to go through.
  Where is our true compassion? If we were able to find any speck of empathy within our souls, we would quickly sacrifice what we Americans so often cling to—time, money, refuge, and our self-absorbed fears. However, our shallow comforts as well as our

privilege of apathy are taking precedent over the lives of others.

If it truly mattered to us, our outrage over Aylan Kurdi's lifeless body on the beach or the heart-wrenching footage of Omran Daqneesh alone in an ambulance bleeding in shock, would have led us to action. Our entire world was so outraged, right? Yet how many pursued love?

How many more children have to be needlessly slaughtered for us to decide their lives actually matter? Are our hearts so hard that the death of small children doesn't inflict true compassion in us? In the self-proclaimed Christian nation of the world, why has apathy overruled the ways of Jesus' bold love of the other?

American Christians, please tell me why you look nothing like your Savior who doesn't love based on nationality, race, or religion. Please, tell me why you are exclusive to the point that the most vulnerable needlessly suffer and are being slaughtered. Please help me understand why you choose apathy, comfort, and self-absorption over the Great Command of Jesus. Please help me understand why my beautiful, joyful nine-year-old Syrian friend could lose her life tomorrow and the picture of her dead body would be but a vague moment of sadness in your day.

As you hail your president for bombing an Assad airbase, ask yourself, is this how we love those who have suffered immeasurably? Don't forget that it was but a handful of days ago that this same president authorized airstrikes killing yet more innocent Syrian children.

Don't be fooled: compassion elicits kindness, not revenge. True compassion toward these beautiful children would be simple enough as offering our hand, offering a place of refuge, not more bombs, not more war. I wish we could see the humanity that we are missing, how much these lives truly matter. I wish it mattered like it matters to the one you call Savior, the guy who always loved first, the most radical peacemaker in history. I wish we weren't too afraid to embrace the way of bold love. I wish we would let love win.

* * *

It is not just refugees halfway around the world seeking refuge; there are people seeking safety and opportunity much closer to home, on our own nation's southern border.

White-Jesus exclusivism is on full display when its leader can come to power by promising to build a literal wall to keep immigrants out, and to take families who are originally from south of the border and have lived their entire lives in the U.S., and send them back to a country that is no longer their own. In 2017, during the first 100 days after Trump signed executive orders "cracking down" on immigration, there were close to 11,000 arrests—over a 150 percent increase from 2016—of completely innocent immigrants, and the numbers are only increasing.[1] As for the wall, prototypes are being made as Trump tries to leverage the Deferred Action for Childhood Arrivals act (DACA), which allows 800,000 people who came illegally to the U.S. as children to stay, to try to get the approval for the billions and billions of dollars to start building the actual wall. And despite Trump's promises, Mexico will not be paying.

The White-Jesus Christian agenda these days is to have ICE teams hunt immigrants who have committed no crime but seeking a better life for their families. I don't know about you, but if I needed to flee my home country in order to give my kids a decent life, I would do it in a heartbeat. You probably would too. And—I would think—so would those who support these harsh immigration policies.

That may be easy to forget when you're not the one watching your kids suffer, but it doesn't make the hurtful behavior excusable. I once had a conversation with a woman who I perceived to be incredibly kind and caring, but when the topic of immigration was brought up, compassion was nowhere to be found.

"You know, Trump just wants to get rid of the criminals," she said.

"So why is ICE imprisoning entire families that have lived here their entire lives and never committed a crime?" I asked.

"Well, if they are here illegally, they are committing a crime," she said.

"So what you are telling me is that those here illegally who were simply seeking a decent life for their children and have done nothing wrong but work their ass off to make a life here, should be kicked out? And their children too, if they were not born on our soil?" I asked her with a sort of fabricated confusion.

"We need a better legal path to immigration so those types of families can come legally, but we can't just let people in," she responded.

I certainly agree we need a better path to immigration,

but if people are seeking a better life, doing valuable work that contributes to our society, and not hurting anyone, why the hell would we want to throw them out? Because they are not here legally? Becoming "legal" is one of their greatest desires, but we have made it almost impossible. Why do we think that Jesus would be okay with us finding those without papers—especially those who are simply seeking refuge—and incarcerating and deporting them? On any front of this entire topic of inclusion/exclusion, or really any topic in the entire universe, why would we think the way of Jesus would be anything but love?

Let's be real, if we are going to follow the refugee Messiah of the red letters, we must welcome the stranger, particularly those in the most need, regardless of their country of origin. I mean, look at the story of the Good Samaritan that we have talked about a few times. It was the foreigner who extended mercy; it was the foreigner who loved. And it was Jesus who specifically said, go and do the same. The foreigner is the "sheep" in this story, the one about whom we are told to "go and do likewise," extending love to people in need, even when they are not like us.

Let's talk about a story that embodies the sheep life vs. the goat life. There are some really awesome organizations that are taking gallons of water and supplies and leaving it in the desert along different migrant paths north of the Mexican border. They are going out of their way to seek out the vulnerable, the "least of these," and loving them as Jesus would. They are literally giving a drink to the thirsty. Amazing right?

What is crazy is that what these groups are doing is actually not legal. In this self-proclaimed "Christian" nation, it is not legal to leave water, in the desert heat, for undocumented immigrants. There are actually people, some of whom are U.S. border patrol, who go and dump any water that was left. Not only are they goat people by not welcoming the stranger, they are actively working against the sheep people who are simply following the ways of Jesus!

Jesus didn't discriminate. He would have been at the border handing out water in a heartbeat—which reminds me of something Jesus once did:

> After Jesus had finished all his sayings in the hearing of the people, he entered Capernaum. A centurion there had a slave whom he valued highly, and who was ill and close to death.
>
> When he heard about Jesus, he sent some Jewish elders to him, asking him to come and heal his slave. When they came to Jesus, they appealed to him earnestly, saying, "He is worthy of having you do this for him, for he loves our people, and it is he who built our synagogue for us."
>
> And Jesus went with them, but when he was not far from the house, the centurion sent friends to say to him, "Lord, do not trouble yourself, for I am not worthy to have you come under my roof; therefore I did not presume to come to you. But only speak the word, and let my servant be healed.
>
> "For I also am a man set under authority, with soldiers under me; and I say to one, 'Go,' and he goes, and to another, 'Come,' and he comes, and to my slave, 'Do this,' and the slave does it."
>
> When Jesus heard this he was amazed at him, and turning to the crowd that followed him, he said, "I tell you, not even in Israel have I found such faith."

When those who had been sent returned to the
house, they found the slave in good health.

Luke 7:1–10

There are so many interesting things about this
story: the humility of the centurion, the compassion of
Jesus, and Jesus' amazement of this guy's faith are all worth
exploring. But most remarkable is that Jesus didn't simply help a random nice guy. Jesus helped a guy who was
part of an oppressive occupation of his people. Yeah, the
guy may have been one of the nicer Roman soldiers, but
he was still an occupying soldier. As far as the Jews were
concerned, I doubt this guy had taken a legal path to
occupancy.

Regardless, Jesus didn't declare the Roman centurion unworthy of help, or call for the expulsion of the
Romans from the land of his people. He extended mercy
and love to the centurion and his servant, and praised him,
declaring that the foreign man's faith was greater than that
of anyone in Israel.

To be honest, I have seen more faith from those who
do not call themselves Christians than from most of those
who claim to follow Jesus. I have learned more about what
red-letter love looks like when in the middle of a Muslim
country than I have right here in the U.S.

The first time (and every time after) that I was for-
tunate enough to travel to the Syrian border I met some of
the most amazing humans. I am an introvert, and I can fully
admit that I can sometimes be super awkward when I meet
people, or at least inwardly I feel awkwardly uncomfortable. However, when I am in this place that my culture tells
me I am supposed to be afraid to go to, I have never felt
anything but the most incredible hospitality. The kind of

hospitality that welcomes strangers as family, melting away even an introvert's innate fear of small talk. I met a ton of awesome people, but there was one family in particular that stole my heart.

This family of six graciously welcomed us into their home, which was filled with warmth, joy, kindness, love, and constant smiles. We drank tea and simply hung out like we were old friends. The four young children drew beautiful pictures in my small notebook and giggled at my poor attempt to speak Arabic. Their young, shy son had the most joyful smile and wild facial expressions, reminding me so much of my own son; this sweet boy melted my heart, and we quickly became buddies. The father drew an on-point picture of a certain world "leader" and the mother had the most kind and gentle spirit. Her eyes told a story of a journey through the most horrific circumstances, yet her smile and embrace were that of pure kindness and love.

Like countless other Syrian families, this family lost everything when they fled the war. Though they made it to Jordan, they are not allowed to work in country (if they are caught working, they are sent back to Syria, a likely death sentence). Their family is scattered around the world and they long to go home—an impossible desire at the time. They have faced and seen the unimaginable with stories that would shatter your heart—stories that will never stop shattering mine. After all the hurt and suffering this family has experienced and as we have turned our backs—they have every reason and are completely justified to be mad at the world, yet there was not an ounce of bitterness in this household.

Before we left, the oldest girl, who was eight and only had a couple of toys in a small purse, pulled out a sparkling green bead and told me she wanted me to have it. My heart was done. This gift touched my soul like nothing I have ever received. This amazing little girl had almost nothing, yet she chose to give, simply out of pure kindness and love. We Americans often struggle to be generous out of our abundance, fearful that sharing with others might leave us without enough—and this child gave out of the little she had. Her gift was a lesson of true sacrificial love that we could all stand to learn from. This awesome family, this amazing little girl—they are the same people whom our White-Jesus nation wants to refuse refuge to. We call them terrorists and refuse our hand when we have all the means (and would be privileged) to welcome them with open arms.

The world tries to say I am their enemy, yet they embraced us with a kindness and warmth to a depth that I have never experienced domestically. They chose to love anyway. When Jesus says to love others, it looks like welcoming strangers—"the other"—into your home with kindness and tea. It means joyfully giving away your treasure out of the love in your heart, even when you have nothing yourself. It is genuine, it is kind, it is bold, and it has no other motive but love.

This is the love that changes the world. This is the love of the red-letter Jesus. Do we want to love like this, or do we ignore the hurt that surrounds us as we stay consumed with ourselves? Do we want to live our lives as sheep people or goat people? It's our call. It's your call.

Chapter 11

MAKING WAR, NOT PEACE
Violence

Today as I sit in a coffee shop in the middle of a rainy day in Iowa, what floods my mind as well as my newsfeed is yet another mass shooting in this self-proclaimed Christian nation.

This definitely isn't the first time some angry white guy has unloaded rounds of bullets on random unsuspecting victims: we've seen it in churches, movie theaters, even elementary schools—yet the general response to the horrific gun violence tends to be more guns. You know, the eye-for-an-eye, solve violence with violence type of logic.

As you may know, White-Jesus Christianity is a major advocate of gun rights. It's as if the Second Amendment was implemented by God on a stone tablet, burning bush style. It's definitely a few hundred steps above the Great Commandment in the book of White-Jesus. I mean it is only logical that we need the right to protect ourselves; that's what Jesus would do, right? Because we have seen time and time again Jesus advocate for self-protection.

Seriously, there were many times when crowds got pissed at something Jesus said and were all about killing him, and so Jesus stood his ground and physically defended himself like any good American would do. Except that he actually didn't. He didn't stand his ground and never met violence with violence, not even in self-defense.

So if Jesus didn't stand his ground, what did he do?

There were plenty of times J made people mad enough that they wanted to legit kill him on the spot. Remember the time when Jesus unrolled a scroll at a synagogue and read a passage that basically said he was the guy the people had been waiting for and the people were like, "Yay, he is going to make Israel great again"? And then J basically crushed their nationalist dreams as he casually let them know that this good news was also for non-Jews and they didn't want to share so, "When they heard this, all in the synagogue were filled with rage. They got up, drove him out of the town, and led him to the brow of the hill on which their town was built, so that they might hurl him off the cliff. But he passed through the midst of them and went on his way" (Luke 4:28–30).

Wow! They wanted to "hurl him off a cliff." That's some Negan (from the *Walking Dead*) kind of insane. How Jesus managed to just walk right through them and leave is pretty crazy.

There was another time that some people accused Jesus of having a demon, and so Jesus of course set them straight because that's not a nice accusation, and he pretty much just roasted these guys by suggesting that they don't even know the God they call God.

"So they picked up stones to throw at him, but Jesus hid himself and went out of the temple" (John 8:59).

He just slipped on out of there!

Then there was another time that people accused Jesus of blasphemy and making himself God, and they tried to arrest him right then and there, "but he escaped from their hands. He went away again across the Jordan to the place where John had been baptizing earlier, and he remained there" (John 10:39–40).

There is a theme here—Jesus says stuff that makes
people mad, he doubles down, throwing out some sarcastic
or smartass shade, and then people rage and want to murder him, but he simply bounces away without drawing a
weapon or physically defending himself in any way. Crazy,
right? I could be way off, but according to the red letters, it
is almost as if Jesus' position was essentially the exact opposite of "stand your ground." He truly was nonviolent, even
in situations of self-defense.

I know, I know, but what about the time that Jesus
said this to his boys?

"When I sent you out without a purse, bag, or sandals, did you lack anything?" They said, "No, not a
thing." He said to them, "But now, the one who has
a purse must take it, and likewise a bag. And the one
who has no sword must sell his cloak and buy one.
For I tell you, this scripture must be fulfilled in me,
'And he was counted among the lawless'; and indeed
what is written about me is being fulfilled." They
said, "Lord, look, here are two swords." He replied,
"It is enough."

Luke 22:35–38

So I get that we could take this and be like, "See,
Jesus is telling his boys to weapon up," but I honestly don't
think that's what is truly going on here.

For one, Jesus is known for speaking in code through
parables and metaphors. I mean, right before he said all of
this, we can read that J was talking about his boys eating
his body and drinking his blood, which I am almost a hundred percent positive was to be taken as symbolism, not
literally. So being as Jesus was not into violence, even in

self-defense, it is pretty possible this was also meant to be symbolic, warning them to be prepared to be strong and able to follow his ways without him physically with them. Not like, "Hey guys, you need to take some self-defense classes or whatever, cause when I am gone, you will need them."

And because his boys often didn't catch the metaphors, they got all excited like and said, "Yeah, look we've got two swords J, we are good, right?"

And then Jesus was like, "That's enough" as in "This conversation is over because you are not getting it . . . again."

It's hard to say; this story has been debated since its existence, but shortly after the whole sword conversation, we see a major example of Jesus being nonviolent in a manner that would contradict the idea that he was talking about the need for a weapon of self-defense.

> While he [Jesus] was still speaking, suddenly a crowd came, and the one called Judas, one of the twelve, was leading them. He approached Jesus to kiss him; but Jesus said to him, "Judas, is it with a kiss that you are betraying the Son of Man?" When those who were around him saw what was coming, they asked, "Lord, should we strike with the sword?" Then one of them struck the slave of the high priest and cut off his right ear. But Jesus said, "No more of this!" And he touched his ear and healed him. Then Jesus said to the chief priests, the officers of the temple police, and the elders who had come for him, "Have you come out with swords and clubs as if I were a bandit? When I was with you day after day in the temple, you

did not lay hands on me. But this is your hour, and the power of darkness!"

Luke 22:47–53

If there was ever a time to retaliate using violence in self-defense, this would have been it. But Jesus clearly wanted none of it.

So I am just seriously confused as to how the Second Amendment and White-Jesus' commitment to the NRA could be seen to reflect the red letters in any way. Is there truly anything other than contradictions here? Do we ever see Jesus condone violence? Maybe we need to reevaluate ourselves and the priority we place on self-protection that overcomes our priority to follow the ways of Jesus.

* * *

If you have not noticed, this White-Jesus nation is infatuated with war, fueled by a fabricated notion that there is a constant threat to our safety. Do you even remember the last time America didn't have some major enemy we were supposed to be constantly afraid of because they were threatening our freedom as if our world was Gotham City? If you are alive and breathing right now, it was probably before your lifetime.

Let's talk a bit of history. You see, in order to understand why the world is the way it is today, we need to have some understanding of our past. We need to be able to recognize the warning signs of the empowerment of fascism and fight it before it starts. Or fight it after it starts, if we ignore all the signs of history and actually let a sociopath become the leader of our country.

In 1950, the National Security Council presented Truman with a top-secret document (that has since been declassified so you can check this craziness out for yourself) called NSC-68.[1] Now this document is a big deal, basically outlining a plan for how our government could hype up an enemy for the American people to fear in order to create a fabricated justification to keep military spending high after World War II. You see, we were manufacturing giants during the war, and we weren't about to lose that cash flow.

Initially, our scary enemy was the Soviets, and you guys, the propaganda about the supposed communist threat to America did not quite match the actual threat level those reds actually caused. There was a bit—okay a ton—of exaggeration, which our government was well aware of. After the Soviet Union collapsed and the Cold War ended, we needed a new threat to keep the people good and fearful, supporting massive military spending even when we aren't officially at war. So it worked out that our big threat shifted from scary, baby-eating communists to Middle Eastern terrorists.

The Reagan administration—elected by courting White-Jesus Christians away from the first actual red-letter-Jesus-following president, Jimmy Carter—developed an idea that has shaped much of our policy and is deeply embedded into our current way of life: Peace through strength.

Basically, the idea is that if we have the biggest, baddest military, we will have peace because no one will mess with us. I mean, it sort of sounds logical, except that the truth is that the concept of peace through strength doesn't work in the least. According to the Stockholm International Peace Research Institute in 2016, the U.S. ranked number one (not a great thing to be the greatest at) in military spending at $611 billion.[2] Guess what we were ranked for peace? The Global Peace Index (GPI) rates a country's peacefulness based on three factors: societal safety and security, the extent of ongoing conflict both domestically and abroad, and international conflict and the depth of militarization. According to the GPI, we were ranked 114th in peace.[3] Oh, and our military budget is still climbing, moving on up, and our level of peace isn't getting any better. "Peace through strength" is really just another dumb rationale to continue to increase our military budget while keeping the support of the general public by keeping them constantly terrified. We are both personally and as a nation so wrongly obsessed with a fabricated need for self-protection.

Let me bring a bit more perspective, again according to the Stockholm International Peace Research Institute: just 10 percent of the 2015 world's military budget of about 1.7 trillion dollars could end poverty by 2030.[4] That's about 170 billion dollars—less than a third of the U.S.'s 2016 military budget alone. Think about that. While Jesus did not prioritize self-protection, especially by the means of weapons, he did place a pretty high priority on feeding the hungry, and yet White-Jesus Christianity won't reduce our national military spending to accomplish that goal.

Jesus doesn't care about our desire for security first— Jesus cares about loving others, even when it means sacrificing our own security and comfort. Regardless of the fact that, because of a ton of propaganda, we may feel we need military strength to save this life we cling to, Jesus said, "those who want to save their life will lose it, and those who lose their life for my sake will find it" (Matt. 16:25).

And then there was that time Jesus said that those who live by the sword die by the sword (Matt. 26:52). Honestly y'all, ours is a nation that worships the sword. White-Jesus

Christianity is a religion that is far more focused on living by the gun than living by the red letters, and Jesus told us where that ends.

* * *

What makes this nation's love of weapons and idolatry of national security not just sad but ironic is that many of those same people who make excuses for violence also loudly and proudly call themselves pro-life. For White-Jesus Christians, however, this term only applies to the issue of abortion, and one's position on this one issue becomes the driving question behind many people's choice of leaders. My point here is not to debate the morality of abortion, but to point out the hypocrisy of valuing life in one circumstance while so flagrantly disregarding it in many others. White-Jesus pro-birth warriors—even the ones who aren't just pro-life on the streets and pro-choice in the sheets, convincing their mistresses to have secret abortions—are supporting a ridiculous amount of policy that contradicts their claimed value of innocent life. The hypocrisy between the claim to value pre-birth life and the clear lack of value of post-birth life casts doubt on their entire worldview.

You see, this is the same faction that resists any limitation on their right to own assault weapons; supports a Muslim ban to refuse refuge to the most vulnerable; fights adamantly against universal healthcare; supports drone strikes that kill thousands of children abroad, labeling them "collateral damage"; and tends to justify police brutality, even murder, against people of color. There is not a lot of fighting for the right to life going on there. Basically, after they are out of the birth canal, people are on their own.

It's almost as if the value is not in life itself, but in the idea of appearing righteous in the stance of "pro-life" because really, it's easy to argue that abortion is wrong without any sort of perceived personal costs. When White-Jesus Christians picket abortion clinics and call young women murderers, they lose nothing. There is no personal cost. It's not like they are out there offering these young, terrified women who feel there is no other option another way out. They don't actually have to do anything; they are sacrificing nothing.

If we claim all life is precious and actually mean it, we should be willing to make sacrifices so that others can have things like clean drinking water, food, shelter, breath in their lungs—instead of cutting funding for children's health-care programs so that billionaires can get a tax cut. It's hard to argue that you are pro-life if you are also campaigning against social welfare programs like affordable housing, food assistance, and free daycare—things that give people who are in a tough spot a chance at being able to successfully parent a child.

Even if the passion of your soul lies on the issue of abortion, your votes are undermining the very goal you are striving for. We can't stand behind people who will take away free contraceptives and then wonder why the abortion rate climbs. If we can picket an abortion clinic but won't offer a dime to help give young women a chance to either prevent the situation in the first place or fight to enable a system that will allow them to be able to parent successfully, then we're not even pro-life when it comes to abortion. We are not even really pro-birth.

While people give lip service to reducing the abortion rate, we are watching children die on our TV screens, shot with semi-automatic rifles in their classrooms. Unarmed people of color killed by police officers livestreams to our social media. U.S. drone strikes kill hundreds of civilians. And what is the White-Jesus response? Is it to make it more difficult for people to obtain assault weapons, or hold authorities accountable for their crimes, or attempt to slow the violence? No, the response is to militarize our children's teachers by giving them guns, justifications of the killing of people of color, and excusing the children who die from our drone strikes as "collateral damage." It's a continual allowance of violence that kills the innocent of our country every day. Why aren't their lives precious enough to fight for? Why does White-Jesus Christianity excuse and sometimes even advocate for policies that only increase violence? If the red-letter Jesus is bold love, why is White-Jesus America so violent?

Chapter 12
LIVING THE DREAM
Consumerism

We're all familiar with the American Dream—our culture's idea of a successful life, measured by the amount of material items we can stockpile before death. This celebrated social ideal tells us the main purpose of life is to work our ass off to make good money so that we can accumulate a lot of stuff and die comfortably with a shallow empire of consumerist wealth.

Not only is this mentality immersed into our mass-commercialized, capitalist, red-white-and-blue culture, it's woven into the ideology of the White-Jesus Church. This is troubling because Jesus had basically nothing in terms of material items.

Regardless, it's not hard to find multi-millionaire mega pastors capitalizing on preaching the prosperity gospel—the idea that it's God's desire to financially bless his followers depending on the strength of their faith and, you know, the amount they donate to mega churches and televangelists. These preachers, in turn, because they have pleased God, are able to buy multi-million-dollar homes, private jets, and other luxury items. If that were Jesus' philosophy, he and his buddies would have had Bill Gates' sort of cash flow.

First, let me preface this conversation with the fact that there is nothing wrong at all with being financially well off. It would just seem that the more money we have, the more Jesus would like us to use our abundance to love others. And this does not always seem to be the case.

When I was a young adult, I once attended a Sunday Easter service with my family at a fairly popular church in the Houston area. So on this special day, one of the most highly attended services of the year, the pastor starts talking about an additional offering that the church needed for this super urgent and important project. So maybe they were raising money for something like a housing project for the homeless or feeding the poor or job training programs, one of those loving-others type of things that churches are "supposed" to do. Yeah, they weren't.

Rather, they needed some extra cash money to buy new chairs for their large auditorium. Chairs that would cost over $200 apiece. The pastor actually told us the cost of each chair.

I remember thinking "Is this guy flipping for real? I wonder how many people they could have put through college with half the amount of their new chair budget." My issue is not with the chairs themselves, but with the fact that this church was so focused on building its own material kingdom, improving its already-posh facilities, even on Easter Sunday, when we are supposedly celebrating Jesus' triumph over the ways of the world.

To be real with you, this White-Jesus mentality of collecting money at church to reinvest into your own comfort reminds me of that time Jesus "fashioned some whips."

It was close to the time of Passover and Jesus was down hanging out in Jerusalem. He decided to head over to the temple courts to see what was going on and to his dismay, to put it lightly, he found people selling livestock and doves, and others chilling at tables exchanging money.

(See John 2:13-17.) When Jesus saw this he was pissed, like in a hard-core holy manner.

So what did Jesus do? Well, he simply made himself a whip and flipped some tables like a boss. He used the whip to drive out the animals. (Let's be clear, it was *not* to whip people. He was clearly super pissed, but he was not physically violent. He didn't hurt people.) He flipped over the tables of the money changers Indiana Jones-style and said something like, "Get these out of here! Stop using my father's house for money to buy yourselves purple-leather-movie-theater-style chairs. Stop turning my Father's house into a damn mall!"

Now, I am going to assume the profits from the sales in the temple courts were not going to feed the homeless or care for the sick. Had they been doing a local fundraiser for widows and orphans, I doubt Jesus would have flipped out.

To be real, I feel like when the majority of a church's budget goes toward upgrading a fancy building as a priority over loving the vulnerable, there is a problem. When churches put more effort into consumerist vanity than loving others, they have fallen into the fabricated idea that the success of their church is based on the same mentality of the American Dream: work hard, fill seats, bring in more tithes, buy a bigger building, fill more seats, start more programs like a singles club, upgrade the lasers in the auditorium, fill more chairs, bring in more tithes, hold a national conference and get those Hillsong people there, bring more tithes, buy more land, build a pretty prayer building, start a school that specializes in the enneagram, bring in more tithes, and repeat.

It's as if the success of many American churches is measured by how abundantly bourgeois their building is and how full their sanctuary stays on Sunday morning as they worship with a sound system that cost more than my house. Basically, the successful church in White-Jesus Christianity is the one that has the most stuff. Let's be honest with each other, it would seem that if Jesus got mad at people selling stuff in the temple courts for their own means, I doubt he would be down with churches taking money to buy fancier crap as they fall into a sort of religious consumerist agenda over the great agenda of Jesus—loving others authentically.

* * *

The American Dream mentality affects pretty much all of us, to some extent. The sad reality is that we all struggle to resist the tempting belief that more stuff equals more happiness. Billions of dollars a year are spent on convincing us that to be happy, we need more random crap. I mean, why do we need to spend almost a thousand dollars on a brand-new iPhone twice a year when a perfectly good Android won't constantly run out of storage (sorry Apple people)? The point is, we don't need the newest phone every few months just because the selfie camera may have slightly better filter effects. It won't bring us the life fulfillment we are hoping for.

In following the ways of Jesus, we can pretty much be completely confident that a life of consumerism doesn't align with the red letters. J literally talked about not falling into a life of materialism when he said something like, "Hey guys, don't store up all of this cheap, material plastic crap on earth, where moths and vermin will eat holes in your brand new Michael Kors purse and thieves will steal the expensive rims off your Audi that you spent your life savings on. Y'all store up treasure in heaven where it cannot be jacked or destroyed. Where your treasure is, your heart will also be. Point blank." (See Matt. 6:19–21.) And then I imagine a mic drop, but that's beside the point.

Jesus, even back in his day before Facebook ads and million-dollar commercials, was fully aware of how easy it could be to fall into a life of chasing material wealth over following his ways of radical generosity and sacrificial love. He might as well have said that chasing the American Dream as a way of life ensures that your heart will be lost in a soul-sucking quest for a shallow empire of crap.

Seriously think about it: Where truly is your treasure? Where truly is your heart?

I would like to imagine that I am on a path toward minimalist-ish living and letting go of the American Dream of wealth and security while I always love sacrificially first. But to be honest, I have a long way to go. I'm not in the least immune to the innate desire to buy out Target.

But I have had some victories in the fight. For instance, a few years ago, I had a giant walk-in closet overflowing with hundreds of clothing items. I mean, I tried to justify it by the fact that 95 percent of the clothes I bought came from trendy thrift stores and therefore supported the local economy and not the slave labor of big corporations, but the fact was I always wanted, even felt like I needed, more boots or off-the-shoulder sweaters. Like if I had this item I desired, something inside me would be complete, I would be able to feel at rest.

My husband, on the other hand, is into this minimalist clothes thing. He essentially has a uniform that is a limited amount of clothing items that he can just throw on without really thinking. Apparently Mark Zuckerberg does the same thing, and he basically runs the world. Rich tried to convince me that this approach to clothing was "freeing." But let's be real, there was no way I could only have a few go-to clothing items, I mean, what if something came up and I needed that tie-die maxi skirt?

Now if I am going to be honest with you, out of my giant kingdom of clothes, I pretty much always wore the same five items 80 percent of the time. And at some point I realized that trying on multiple outfits to see what I felt good in, only to end up in the exact same style that I wore every day, was not the best way to spend half an hour.

So slowly I gave in and began to clear out my closet in an effort to get to a place where I could be content with less. That was the goal. And you know what? This small attempt at letting go of a little part of my own consumerist mentality *was* incredibly freeing. I now have a tiny closet, and I actually feel really good about it. It's as if this small and pretty shallow change has led to a deeper realization of the fact that the opposite of consumerism is what leads to true contentment.

The truth becomes pretty obvious, if we look beneath the layers of our deeply unnecessary wants, that the consumerist mentality pretty much revolves around two key factors: greed and money. Maybe that's why Jesus said that we "cannot serve both God and wealth" (Luke 16:13). And mind you, when he said this, it pissed off the religious elite type of his day, as they were point blank greedy and money hungry. I'm sure you've seen the modern equivalent of this type:

> The Pharisees, who were lovers of money, heard all this, and they ridiculed him. So he said to them, "You are those who justify yourselves in the sight of oth-

ers; but God knows your hearts; for what is prized by
human beings is an abomination in the sight of God."
Luke 16:14–15

I don't know if my overstuffed closet was an abomination to God, but I'm pretty sure the financial security
I pursued so desperately as a young, single mom was. It
was not just a priority, but my number one priority. Like
many Americans, especially those of us who had some odds
against us, the dream of financial security was my number
one goal. Yet, when I finally reached that place of security that I worked so hard for, I realized that there was no
true life in that quest. Just more wanting. So, with much
apprehension and a ton of anxiety, I decided to give up my
secure, stable teaching job to try and focus on a life of loving
others first. Naturally, I had a lot of people, many of whom
are Christians, tell me that I was not being "smart."

But let's be real—if we look at the life of Jesus, he lived
in a manner that would scare the crap out of us Westerners. He basically had nothing: no savings, no property, no
401(k), nothing. I mean nothing in the sense that he didn't
even have the simplest of worldly security and the thing
was, he was totally chill about it. He didn't say, "Go build
a good life, buy a nice home and hold on to your wealth
tightly just in case. You can never save too much, you need
to be smart with your money, an emergency could happen
at any time." If we're being honest, we justify a lot of our
wealth as needed for a just-in-case scenario.

The reality of Jesus is that he often called his followers to pretty much be what we Americans would see as
financially irresponsible. He sent people out with simply
the clothes on their backs, no food, no change of clothes,

and he specifically told them not to bring money. On top of it all, they didn't even have a place to stay; they were supposed to stay in the homes of strangers who would hypothetically welcome them (Luke 9:1–6).

In addition, how many people did Jesus call off of their job site to follow him?

People—especially White-Jesus Christians—would talk some kind of mess if we made these sorts of life moves, even if we were doing it to follow the same guy they call their Savior. I doubt Dave Ramsey would be down with giving away every asset you have and becoming voluntarily homeless.

Notice, though, it's not money in general that is the actual problem, it's our greed of wealth and selfish nature; it's the refusal to use what we have to sacrificially love others first. Sacrificing what we would call the American Dream in order to follow Jesus with everything might be one of the most difficult and boldly countercultural moves we could make.

* * *

If you are still questioning whether the American Dream of consumerism truly contradicts the ways of Jesus, or if I am wildly exaggerating—which, let's be real, could be a slight possibility—let's look at yet another story from Jesus.

> Someone in the crowd said to him, "Teacher, tell my brother to divide the family inheritance with me." But he said to him [probably with some sarcasm], "Friend, who set me to be a judge or arbitrator over you?" And he said to them, "Take care! Be on your

guard against all kinds of greed; for one's life does not consist in the abundance of possessions."

Then he told them a parable [because parables are awesome]:

"The land of a rich man produced abundantly. And he thought to himself, 'What should I do, for I have no place to store my crops?' Then he said, 'I will do this: I will pull down my barns and build larger ones, and there I will store all my grain and my goods. And I will say to my soul, "Soul, you have ample goods laid up for many years; relax, eat, drink, be merry."'

But God said to him, 'You fool! This very night your life is being demanded of you. And the things you have prepared, whose will they be?' So it is with those who store up treasures for themselves but are not rich toward God."

Luke 12:13–21

So this rich guy pretty much says he is set for life now that he has a bunch of stuff saved, and he can basically chill, eat, drink, and be merry (whatever that looks like) and his very soul will be happy. Or so he thinks . . .

How did God respond? Did God applaud him for achieving the American Dream? ("Save up so you can kick back and enjoy" is the same ideology that is deeply ingrained in our red, white, and blue culture, right?) Nope. God point blank called him out. God clearly wasn't about that life. He told the rich guy, "You're dumb. Sorry to tell you but you're going to die, tonight actually, and then where will all of your useless crap be?"

Really, where will all your useless crap go when you

die? Is that really where you want your heart to be throughout your entire life?

Maybe the question shouldn't be: How can I obtain a lot of money to buy a lot of stuff that I think will make me happy and comfortably add to my empire of material wealth that will leave no positive mark on this world? Maybe the question should be: How can I use what I have to sacrificially love others first? Maybe we could put our heart in living out bold love over our facade of egocentric wealth. You know, kind of like Jesus did. Maybe simply asking ourselves these sorts of questions regularly will keep us in check with where our heart truly is and where we want it to be.

We were made for more than a life of building a small consumerist empire in order to die comfortably. There is so much more to our existence than the "American Dream." True life doesn't come from the ability to buy a '68 Mustang or a bunch of new Nikes that were made with slave labor. True life comes from that radical generosity we see in the ways of Jesus who always, sacrificially, loved others first.

Chapter 13

NOT HERE FOR YOUR ENJOYMENT
Misogyny

It's been a long time since the Nineteenth Amendment was passed, like a hundred-ish years (depending on when you are reading this). But while women have had the vote for a century, misogyny still runs as deep as it ever did in the red, white, and blue.

When we think about misogyny, what comes to mind right away? Maybe something like Mark Driscoll and the whole toxic masculinity, the-husband-is-the-head-of-the-household type of complementarian crap, which is incredibly oppressive toward females and basically contradicts every single interaction J had with women in his day. But someone's got to cook supper, do the dishes, fulfill the husband's needs, and raise the children, right?

Another misogynistic ideology that dominates White-Jesus Christianity is what we call purity culture, which seeks to both shame and scare young women out of sex. It's the basic idea that God cares almost as much about a girl's virginity as he does about their salvation, and so they need to stay "pure" until marriage by any means possible or they are essentially damaged goods and no godly man will want to marry a "used" woman. This twisted ideology severely warps young women's ideas of sex, convincing them that consensual physical intimacy is something to be ashamed of.

In White-Jesus youth groups all over the nation this ideology is being taught to young women, sometimes even with props. It might go something like this:

"Check out this glass of cold, refreshing water. Look at it! It's clean, free of impurities, and an amazing treat on a hot summer day. But what happens if I put a few drops of red food dye in it. Whoa, it's no longer clear and free of impurities. What if I add some of this green? Look at that, it's all brown and gross. It's not very appealing is it? I wouldn't want to drink it; would you?

"Your virginity is like that clear glass of water, beautiful when clean but if you defile it even once, it becomes dirty, gross, and unappealing. You can try to add more clean water into the cup, but no matter what, it will still be brown. It can never be pure again!"

There are similar spiels involving chewed gum, cups of spit, and used duct tape. Through all these metaphors, purity culture teaches youth—especially young women—that sex before marriage is the most shameful sin of all. I remember being told on a number of occasions as a young girl, that every time a girl has sex with a boy, she gives him part of her soul that she can never get back. Pieces of her soul are tied to every boy she is impure with, and all she is left with are broken pieces of her soul. It tells women that God and the Christian world values them based on their virginity, not themselves as a person. It's crazy if you look at how the Jesus of the red letters valued women. Jesus didn't care if a woman wasn't "pure."

There was that time when Jesus was in the middle of teaching in a temple court and some religious folk (surprise, surprise) dragged in a woman who was caught in the *act* of adultery (John 8:1–11). Like the actual act. Jesus was asked by these guys what to do with the (probably naked) lady; she straight up broke the law, which clearly said that she should have rocks thrown at her until she dies . . . because that's old school justice . . . but no need to fling rocks at the guy. He is totally fine. It's her fault, right?

Now when the woman was brought over, Jesus sat down and drew in the sand, which I think is awesome. I really wish we knew what he drew or wrote. But I suspect that what he drew wasn't really the point. He showed serious respect by deliberately *not* staring at the naked, terrified, and publically humiliated woman who was probably having the worst day of her life.

Like the badass that he was, Jesus said something along the lines of, "Any of you who are perfect, go ahead and throw a rock."

Clearly no one could say they were perfect, so they all awkwardly left and the woman, who I am sure regardless still was having the worst day of her life, was saved.

This woman was definitely guilty of doing something not very cool. But shaming her while sparing the guy is definitely not cool either, and obviously stoning someone to death (even if it is in your laws) is incredibly messed up. Y'all, not only did Jesus get her off the hook of with the whole rock-death drama, he showed her respect by drawing in the sand instead of staring at her in shame.

The value of a woman does not deplete the more they have sex out of wedlock. And more than that, Jesus made it pretty clear in this story that the level of respect we should all hold for women doesn't lessen in any manner as a result of sexual indiscretions. That's such a ridiculous White-Jesus ideal. The way of the red letters is to see women as the amazing beings they truly are, not as sex objects that need to stay "pure" for their future husbands.

* * *

We probably all know that misogyny runs deeper than just White-Jesus purity culture. Both inside and out of the White-Jesus Chrch, we ladies have pretty much all been made to feel that we are simultaneously too much and not enough. We are called crazy because we are too emotional, not smart enough because our intelligence is threatening, too pretty to be taken seriously or not pretty enough, wearing too much makeup or not enough makeup, too aggressive, too weak, too fat, too thin, too pale, too tan, too outspoken, too timid, the list goes on and on and on. We are raised with this ridiculous ongoing list of what we are supposed to be and not be in order to be valued in our society.

Mainstream, secular Western culture generally doesn't place the focus of women's value on their virginity, but on their outward appearance of sexiness. Our media is flooded with images and portrayals of "sexy" half-naked women because, let's face it, sex sells. Lust sells. Really any objectification of women sells. Our super-sexed culture has taught both women and men that the main value of a woman is based on physical beauty. Every woman has felt the societal pressure to fit a predetermined mold of what is considered attractive. And to make it even more difficult, this mold changes every few years.

I think we all know deep down that placing our inherent value on physical appearances is wrong, but to go deeper, we often have a tendency to mask this cultural-driven vanity and objectification as empowerment. Our society point blank tells women that our sexiness, fitness, and wardrobe are what mark us as a strong, confident, empowered woman. We are taught through a million streams of media that we should feel the best about ourselves when we have visible abs, slim thighs, a pretty face, and a Kardashian ass. And more than that, we need to make sure the world can see it through endless duck-face Instagram posts, because how else will anyone know how valuable we are?

I am absolutely not saying that anything is wrong with posting whatever you want on Instagram. Duck face your little heart out. What I am saying is that we need to think about the societal pressure and the measure of worth of women in our culture as a whole. Even as little girls, most of us grow up obsessing over our appearance in the most ridiculous ways. Weighing ourselves ten times a day, looking at our bodies in the mirror while evaluating every perceived flaw for an hour, binging and purging to stay "fit," spending thousands of dollars to try and fix ourselves to fit the standard definition of beauty. And why? Because we all want the world to value us.

The objectification of women is so ingrained in our society that we often don't see the depth of the lies. And it's not just girls who are being hurt. Boys are taught from a young age to value women based on outward beauty. Through the promotion of the idea that to be a man, they need to be able to score a lot of "hot chicks," lust is ingrained in the idea of manhood, when really this lust is dehumanizing and leads to an innate whisper that women are simply objects to be enjoyed.

It's basically the equally misogynistic flip side to purity culture and its mainstream notion in our society. Both the mainstream oversexualizing of women and the church's purity culture measure women's worth based on their bodies, whether displayed for all to enjoy or kept pure for the enjoyment and ownership of one man, rather than for the people they are. This stuff is everywhere we turn, and if we want to see love win, we need to keep looking at the red letters and focus on how Jesus valued women, especially women that society did not value.

One day, after casting some demons into suicidal pigs, Jesus was heading to the house of Jairus, a local synagogue leader, to help his twelve-year-old daughter who was dying, but before he could get there,

> . . . a large crowd followed him and pressed in on him. Now there was a woman who had been suffering from hemorrhages for twelve years. She had endured much under many physicians, and had spent all that she had; and she was no better, but rather grew worse. She had heard about Jesus, and came up behind him in the crowd and touched his cloak, for she said, "If I but touch his clothes, I will be made well." Immediately her hemorrhage stopped; and she felt in her body that she was healed of her disease. Immediately aware that power had gone forth from him, Jesus turned about in the crowd and said, "Who touched my clothes?" And his disciples said to him, "You see the crowd pressing in on you; how can you say, 'Who touched me?'" He looked all around to see who had done it. But the woman, knowing what had happened to her, came in fear and trembling, fell down before him, and told him the whole truth. He said to her, "Daughter, your faith has made you well; go in peace, and be healed of your disease."
>
> Mark 5:21–34

This woman, who would have been considered unclean in this culture because of the bleeding, was not allowed to touch anyone, especially a man like Jesus. The fact that this woman had been bleeding for twelve years would have made her a social outcast. Because of this, when Jesus asked who touched him, she probably thought she was going to be publically called out, shamed, and humiliated. But when she came forward, that wasn't the case. Jesus didn't see her as unclean. Jesus saw her for who she was; he called her "daughter" and publically affirmed her. This wouldn't have been culturally appropriate, but Jesus humanized the woman, and by healing and affirming her in front of everyone, he publically showed that he valued her and that she was of great value to God. In a culture that was incredibly judgmental, as ours can be today, Jesus loved and valued women boldly even against all cultural norms.

* * *

Objectification of women is pervasive in our culture, and the truth is, it leads to an even darker, more disturbing reality in our world. It leads to rape culture. When I say rape culture, I am not just talking about the high rate of sexual assault and harassment that women face daily, but the more subtle yet systemic discrimination that creates a culture in which sexual assault and harassment are normalized.

In 2006, Tarana Burke coined the term "Me Too" to empower and spread empathy among women of color who had been sexually abused. The idea was popularized and became a broader movement in 2017 when Alyssa Milano told people to tweet the phrase to show the world how big of an issue sexual assault and harassment is for all women. As millions of women who had experienced sexual assault or harassment posted #MeToo to their social media, much of the world was shocked at the number of women that came forward. It was our grandmas, our sisters, our daughters, our idols; it was everywhere and basically everyone.

The thing is, objectifying women is so much the norm, it's become easy to overlook how bad the issue truly is. After experiencing things like being catcalled by grown men as a tween, or being hit on multiple times a day at work by customers that we would get fired for flipping out on, or being expected not to react when random men straight up stare at our body, I think many of us have convinced ourselves that these things are just part of being a woman. We are taught that this kind of treatment shouldn't be that big of a deal.

I always knew rape culture was a real issue, but to be honest, I don't think I realized how deep this issue ran until I began watching the vast numbers of women come forward and share their stories of sexual assault and sexual harassment with #MeToo. I didn't fully realize how many other women had gone through the same sort of abuse that I had and also never said a word. After being sexually assaulted at the age of thirteen, I honestly and sincerely thought it was my fault. I didn't even tell my parents, ever. So many other women have never spoken a word about the rape, sexual assault, or harassment they have experienced, creating a collective silence that is finally being broken, showing us that it's time to start doing something about rape culture.

The fact that we elected a known sexual predator to lead our nation should be a clue as to the depths of dysfunction we are facing. Trump was elected president with the public's full awareness of his record. His ex-wife has claimed that he violently raped her. Over twenty women have claimed he sexually assaulted them. He has admitted that he would regularly walk in the changing rooms at the Miss Universe pageants as the girls were changing. He was caught on tape boasting about sexually assaulting women, saying that because he was rich, he could just kiss any woman he wanted and "grab them by the pussy."[1] With full knowledge of all of this and more, a significant portion of the American public of voting age, who voted in 2016—including most of the White-Jesus American Church—supported this man. It was the purity-obsessed, White-Jesus men (and women!) who defended Trump's talk about sexual assault as simply "locker room talk." What the hell, White-Jesus? Do you think the Jesus of the red letters would be cool with this?

Do you think Jesus would be cool with "locker room" talk or catcalls? Oh, but what about the lust factor? What if a woman dresses sexy? I mean she's causing men to stumble, and that's on her, right? Yeah, not even a little bit, according to Jesus.

"You have heard that it was said, 'You shall not commit adultery.' But I say to you that everyone who looks at a woman with lust has already committed adultery with her in his heart" (Matt. 5:27–28). I could be wrong, but I am pretty sure that Jesus was absolutely opposed to the lustful objectification of women. I mean he straight up told guys that looking is not okay, and I bet locker room talk falls into that same category. Not only did Jesus straight up call men out for objectifying women, he went way out of his way to show respect to women—all women. You know, like that time we just talked about when Jesus drew in the sand instead of shaming the naked, adulterous woman. Jesus treated women as people of value. I mean really, when we look at how Jesus interacted with women, it's almost like he highly respected and cared about women as equals.

For instance, do you know who the first person was that J appeared to after he came back from the world of death (or wherever he was during those three post-death days)? His homie Mary Magdalene, the chick who had been possessed by seven demons and whom Jesus loved and valued deeply.

Here is the scene: Mary shows up at the tomb of Jesus a few days after J died and sees that the stone covering the opening of the tomb is gone. She goes and gets some of his boys, and they take a look and see that J's body is gone and then go home. Mary stays.

> But Mary stood weeping outside the tomb. As she wept, she bent over to look into the tomb; and she saw two angels in white, sitting where the body of Jesus had been lying, one at the head and the other at the feet. They said to her, "Woman, why are you weeping?" She said to them, "They have taken away my Lord, and I do not know where they have laid him." When she had said this, she turned around and saw Jesus standing there, but she did not know that it was Jesus. Jesus said to her, "Woman, why are you weeping? Whom are you looking for?" Supposing him to be the gardener, she said to him, "Sir, if you have carried him away, tell me where you have laid him, and I will take him away." Jesus said to her, "Mary!" She turned and said to him in Hebrew, "Rabbouni!" (which means Teacher). Jesus said to her, "Do not hold on to me, because I have not yet ascended to the Father. But go to my brothers and say to them, 'I am ascending to my Father and your Father, to my God and your God.'" Mary Magdalene went and announced to the disciples, "I have seen the Lord"; and she told them that he had said these things to her.
>
> John 20:1–18

Jesus wouldn't have appeared to Mary first, before any of his bros, if she were not super important to him. He valued her highly, just like he valued all women in a world where women were seen as "less-than." Because women are not less-than; women are awesome.

* * *

In January 2017, something pretty damn awesome happened. Millions of people took to the streets of their cities to protest the bigotry and misogyny of the man inaugurated the day before, making the Women's March altogether the largest peaceful demonstration in the history of basically ever. People all around the world came together and stood in solidarity, uniting against the oppression of women and really all marginalized people. It was a woman-bred movement of peace and definitely one for the textbooks (though I guess it will depend on who writes those textbooks).

Millions standing in the tension, peacefully demanding for the imbedded values and equality of our world to change—that's true empowerment. Thousands of women calling out the sexual assault/harassment they have faced with a simple #MeToo. The men who stand by our side in solidarity, the men who listen, the men who have acknowledged that the way of over-sexualizing women is point blank gross, the men who draw in the sand, the men who teach their sons a better way. The millions who are finally listening and seeing the reality of misogyny and doing something about it.

That is where J would be, standing in solidarity, marching with millions of women, because that's where love would be.

Chapter 14

SQUAD GOALS
The Marginalized

A conservative white pastor, a liberal peacemaker, and Jesus walk into a bar. Who does J have a beer with? The evangelist praising Jesus' name all over town or the social justice advocate lobbying for reform?

Trick question. Neither. He has a beer with the homeless couple he just met outside and invited in.

It's not a big secret that Jesus hung with the marginalized, those his own people wouldn't touch. Those the religious of his day looked down on. If Jesus was in the U.S. today, he probably wouldn't head over to the local mega church. He'd be with those that church people often treat as inferior, those White-Jesus Christianity has marginalized. His buddies would be the same people as they were in his day, those who the religious exclude. The young single moms, the girl walking out of Planned Parenthood, the felons, the poor, the sick, the crowds marching for Black Lives Matter, the teenagers fighting for gun control, the undocumented immigrants, the LGBTQ+ community. Jesus wasn't just super inclusive of everyone—he went out of his way to be with those who White-Jesus Christianity would call "sinners" today.

Sadly, there are far too many marginalized people groups in our world, but we are going to take a closer look at a few, starting with the group that is probably the most excluded by the White-Jesus Church: the LGBTQ+ community.

White-Jesus hates on the LGBTQ+ community with a rather confusingly high level of intensity. To be honest, it's weird how obsessed they are about who other adults choose to have consensual sex with, as if it affects them in any way, shape, or form. It doesn't, and yet their MO is to reject them. Or, they may try to cast the queerness out of them through some sort of barbaric conversion therapy. It's ridiculous and so hurtful, and for what?

Jesus literally said nothing about sexual orientation. There are no red letters about identifying as LGBTQ+ as being any sort of sin. Not one little word. Yet judging by what we see today from White-Jesus Christian's actions, you would think the LGBTQ+ communities were kicking puppies on the daily. When really all they are doing is embracing who God made them to love and be.

This is the level of ridiculous we are on. Let's say you run a delicious bakery and your fabulous wedding cakes are in high demand. But then, say, some people who make you and all of your friends super uncomfortable, like maybe Trekkies (I married one myself, so I am not hating), come in and want to order a cake for their massive Star Trek-themed wedding. The ceremony will be performed in Klingon and everything.

You think about it for a moment, and then you think about how your people feel about Trekkies, and you decide you can't in good faith support this union because you feel it's unnatural. After you turn the couple away and announce your decision to the world, all of your friends praise your bold stance against the unnatural ways of Trekkies. You are sending a clear message that they need to reconsider their Trekkie ways! You are actually saving them, if you really think about it. Seriously, it would be infringing on your rights as a business owner to be forced to condone a lifestyle that goes against the cultural norm of your people, right?

Now, this story is pretty ridiculous. But replace Trekkie with LGBTQ+ and this is the reality of the ways of White-Jesus Christianity.

It actually gets weirder and far worse. White-Jesus Christians, no joke, blame the LGBTQ+ community for natural disasters. Sure, scientists say that the increasing intensity of natural disasters is because of global warming, but what do they know? Even though Jesus never mentioned anything at all about it, White-Jesus ideology "knows" the truth is that the world-wide, record-breaking, devastating natural disasters we are seeing, like major tsunamis, hurricanes, earthquakes, and wild fires, are God's punishment toward the LGBTQ+ community and any allies who aren't super hateful like White-Jesus would be. God forbid we actually believe science and follow the red-letter ways that are inclusive and loving toward every single human in the world.

In 2017, when Hurricane Harvey hit my hometown of Houston and people were losing everything, White-Jesus elitists with major audiences chose not to extend love but to put out statements saying that the reason for the devastation was due to God's punishment on the LGBTQ+ community. Houston had previously had a lesbian mayor, after all.

To make matters worse, at the same time, a group of over 150 well-known evangelical leaders put out what they called the Nashville Statement. In a nutshell, the Nashville Statement listed what they deemed facts of God (that people made up)—that therefore Christians are required to believe—regarding gender identity and sexuality. It was basically another oppressive set of rules geared toward hurting the LGBTQ+ community. In article 10, it even pretty much said if you affirm LGBTQ+ persons, then you are not a true Christian and you are going to hell.[1]

We've got a natural disaster destroying thousands of lives and White-Jesus Christianity is focused on who people have sex with and what their gender identity may be. There is no angle in which that isn't completely messed up. Living a life free to be who God made you to be and love whomever you love is just point blank *not* a sin—but the dehumanizing way White-Jesus Christians treat the LGBTQ+ community most definitely is. We're talking about parents who disown their children and throw them out on the streets if they come out as LGBTQ+. Kids are killing themselves because of the hate and shame that White-Jesus Christianity pours onto the queer community. Exclusion, judgment, and condemnation are not the ways of Jesus when it came to anyone, especially and including the marginalized.

Let's be real for a minute, if God was going to punish anyone with natural disasters or whatever, it would probably be the super religious elite who use God's name to hurt others. These were the people who really pissed off Jesus, the people he called "whitewashed tombs," looking pure and holy on the outside but inside reeking of hypocrisy and hate (Matt. 23:27).

On the other hand, there were a lot of people who Jesus chilled with who were culturally or socially inappropriate for him to hang with: lepers, women, prostitutes, tax collectors, foreigners, and so on. Look at how Jesus treated those who, according to his religious and cultural norms, he shouldn't have even spoken with, those who were deemed the other and therefore less-than. There are many stories that come to mind, but the following is my favorite.

Here is the scene: Jesus and his boys are traveling, and Jesus needs some alone time, so he sits by this well in a little town while his boys go into town to get some food.

"A Samaritan woman came to draw water, and Jesus said to her, 'Give me a drink.'

"The Samaritan woman said to him, 'How is it that you, a Jew, ask a drink of me, a woman of Samaria?'" (John 4:3–9)

Jews and Samaritans were not on good terms, and all the more so, a Jewish man alone speaking to a Samaritan woman alone was point blank culturally wrong on many levels.

So Jesus and the woman chat about God and "living water," which sounds appealing to the woman, and then Jesus casually brings up everything he knows about the woman's past, which amazes her, because how could some rando know this kind of stuff back when there was no such thing as Facebook stalking? And then Jesus reveals to her that he is the Messiah, who both Jews and Samaritans have been waiting for—mic drop! (See John 4:10–26.)

But what really stands out for me in this story is the disciples' reactions when they catch up to Jesus.

> Just then, his disciples came. They were astonished that he was speaking with a woman, but no one said, "What do you want?" or, "Why are you speaking with her?" Then the woman left her water jar and went back to the city.
>
> John 4:27–28

They had seen the guy do crazy miracles; I mean this is the guy who turned water into wine at a wedding party. But for whatever reason it was this instance of him chilling with a Samaritan woman that really threw them off. And if a simple conversation threw them off, it must have been super incredibly inappropriate for Jesus to talk with her one-on-one. Maybe on the same level as if a White-Jesus Christian baker made a cake for a gay wedding, outraging the White-Jesus Christian society. It's funny, though, how the writer points out that nobody asked any questions about Jesus' "astonishing" actions. Maybe, by that point in the game, J's boys had started to figure out that Jesus knew what he was doing and questioning his ways tended to reflect badly on themselves at the end of the day. That's something to remember: questioning Jesus' radical love for others always ends up with us looking like giant jerks.

Jesus didn't care what other people thought was wrong. Jesus didn't tell the Samaritans they were going to hell if they didn't change their ways; he didn't get up and walk away, giving the Samaritan woman a dirty look or trying to talk her into conversion camp. Just like Jesus fully embraced this woman, Jesus would fully embrace the LGBTQ+ community because he loved her and he loves them deeply, and so should we.

* * *

Another major issue of White-Jesus Christianity that J never mentioned is abortion. When it comes to abortion, the entirety of the issue deals with a single philosophical question: When does life start? Is it conception? As soon as there is a heartbeat? During the third trimester? When a baby can hold up its own head outside the womb?

This is a super important question, but the truth is that none of us really know the answer. There is no single human on this earth who knows precisely when life starts.

There is literally no one who can scientifically prove the line between terminating some cells and taking a life. Since we will never know the exact starting point of what we call life, and Jesus said nothing about the topic, let's talk about how White-Jesus Christianity responds to the issue of abortion and how it aligns with what we do know about the ways of the Jesus of the red letters.

When it comes to the treatment of women who have had an abortion, White-Jesus treats them horribly. They yell and scream and call them murderers and yet refuse to do anything to make societal changes that would decrease the rate of abortions. We see incredible shame and condemnation, but no empathy or love, just anger and hate.

I had a childhood friend who found herself scared and young and pregnant. She didn't know how she would be able to support a child, and abortion felt like her only real choice in a world that isn't exactly kind to young single mothers. My friend had grown up around the church; after she had the abortion, words of White-Christian ideology rang in her head, overwhelming her with hurt and sorrow. The accusation that she had murdered her baby taunted her every minute of every day. One evening, my friend could not take it any longer and swallowed a bottle of pills. She was done with life but not successful with her attempt to end it, so after a few days in the hospital, she was released—but the whispers of White-Jesus condemnation continued. Shortly after she returned home, she was by herself one afternoon, found her parents' gun, and shot herself in the chest. As she bled out, the pain in her soul faded. Because White-Jesus Christianity threw stones instead of extending love, my beautiful friend lost her life and the world lost a wonderful human.

At the funeral, I remember a woman from the church that I used to attend spoke about the tragedy of suicide. Tragic, she said, not because my friend was in so much pain that she couldn't see another way out, but because, according to this woman, my friend's decision to end her life separated her from God eternally. It was an incredibly horrible and cruel fabrication.

Shame, condemnation, and damnation—this is the way of White-Jesus. There is no resemblance of the Jesus of the red letters here, there is no love. Regardless of when we believe life starts, Jesus would never have treated my friend as White-Jesus Christians did. Jesus was about compassion and grace. Jesus would have extended love just like he did to everyone else society excluded, condemned, and treated like crap.

You would think that if a young woman found herself with an unplanned pregnancy and decided to have the baby, maybe White-Jesus Christians would be more loving or something since she did what they said was "right" and didn't have an abortion. But let's be real, that's generally not the case.

I was fifteen when I got pregnant. The father, who was twenty, started as a rebound-type thing, and my main attraction to him was that he always had weed and could buy cigarettes and alcohol. And no, this wasn't Alabama. I was living in Canada at the time; the legal age of consent was fourteen years old, which, looking back, was not even a little bit okay.

I grew up in a home where sex wasn't talked about. All I really knew was that I wasn't supposed to have sex until I was married, and by this point in my life, that ship had sailed. I remember the day I found out I was pregnant in great detail. I remember what the sky looked like, the jeans, blue hoodie, and black skate shoes I was wearing, the exact feeling I had right before I found out, and the cigarette I smoked right after. I was just a kid, a bit older than my daughter is today.

There was a youth sexual health clinic downtown that gave free STD tests, pregnancy tests, and free bags of lube and flavored condoms. Sometimes, my best friend and I would go in when we were bored, pretty much for the flavored condoms that, if I am being honest, we generally used to make scented balloons.

One warmish, bright Alberta day we stopped by to get a free pregnancy test and a fun little "gift bag." Neither one of us thought we were pregnant, it was just something to do when we were bored. Get pregnancy tests for funsies.

We had done this before, and generally while I waited for the results I would get a wave of super nervousness regardless of the fact that I was never truly concerned about being pregnant. Strangely, this time I felt totally chill while waiting for the nurse to return with the results.

But it wasn't the same routine this time. This time, when the nurse returned, *she* was the one who looked super nervous, and at that point I knew what was about to come out of her mouth.

"The test came back positive. You are pregnant," she said with some uncomfortable sympathy.

"Oh, okay."

That's all I said.

It felt surreal; I don't think I knew how to feel. I never thought it would happen to me. I mean, yeah sometimes I forgot to take my birth control pills, but the pull-out method is supposed to work really well, right?

Like I said, I was just a kid.

I called the father from the nurse's office and bluntly

let him know and then casually walked out of the office, told my best friend who was in the waiting room and not pregnant, and shot straight for the exit, immediately lighting a cigarette. It wasn't long before the shock wore off and suffocating anxiety overwhelmed me.

To be honest, abortion was definitely a thought; it would have been a hell of a lot easier to pretend that this never happened.

However, coincidently, a few months prior I had randomly found a White-Jesus published graphic pro-life book with pictures in color of cute-looking fetuses and then some fetal body parts that had been sucked out of a womb. It was pretty harsh, so given these images and the fact I grew up hearing that abortion was murder, the thought of abortion did not last very long.

You may think, "Oh, well I guess that book did what it was made to do, scare people out of abortion," and yes, it did do that in my case, but at the same time there weren't any Christian resources on what to do next. It was simply shame-based propaganda. If the game plan is to scare women out of abortions, you'd think White-Jesus Christians would then help girls who made the choice that they screamed was right.

I was sixteen years old when I gave birth in a Canadian hospital that wouldn't give me an epidural, with my best friend, another friend, and my daughter's dad, who immediately went to work after her birth. At the time, I lived with my dad and ex-stepmom; and my dad was on a business trip while my real mom and two sisters lived a million miles away in Texas.

I was pretty clueless and basically alone. Looking back, I pretty much figured out pregnancy from *What to*

Expect When You're Expecting and then parenting from, well, *Gilmore Girls*. That's not an exaggeration.

A few months after my daughter was born, we moved back to Texas and her dad stayed in Canada. I would be lying if I said it wasn't hard to be a sixteen-year-old parent. But having her saved my life, in a sense. I was incredibly wild and rebellious before I had Hayley. I was a mess, but with a child depending on me, for the first time I had some real ambition past partying. So I got my GED, started college, and moved out at seventeen—during what would have been my senior year of high school. I figured out how to work, get my kid health insurance, pay bills, and budget like a boss.

You know, my daughter truly is the best thing that ever happened to me. I am so insanely grateful to be her mom. But after I had my daughter, there was one place in particular that I dreaded going to more than any other. One place that my daughter and I got constant, relentless stares. One place where people made it obvious that they did not approve of my situation. That one place was the White American Church. Those same Christians who screamed that abortion was murder treated me like I was inferior in my basic humanity because I made the decision they advocated for. It's self-righteous hypocrisy at its best.

It's easy to condemn both a woman's choice to have an abortion and her choice not to, when you have no understanding of the results of their decision and you mindlessly follow White-Jesus. However, as we have seen time and time again, that's not the way of the red letters. The Jesus of the red letters would be kind to not only the teen mom but to the girl who had an abortion. He would befriend them without any sort of lecture or judgment. Jesus is never condemnation or shame, Jesus is love. If our actions are not producing love, they are not the way of the red letters.

* * *

Jesus was all inclusive; his squad was the marginalized:

the refugee searching for safety,

the immigrant trying to give his children a better life,

the person of color who society still allows to be treated with brutality,

the girl who society tries to slut shame because she is comfortable with the fact that God also made her a sexual being,

the children slain around the world because of the violent war mentality of our nation,

those who have been demonized because they are unsure of their sexual or gender identity,

those who have hidden under desks while a white guy with an AR-15 shoots their friends in front of their eyes,

the scared girl at Planned Parenthood and the sixteen-year-old mother who can't take her child to the park without condemning looks,

the Veteran with PTSD who, after dedicating his life to America, is deported to a country that is not really his own,

the young boy of color serving a decade in a private prison for a marijuana charge,

the couple on the side of the road in the rain with a cardboard sign.

These are the people who Jesus loves deeply.

With the White-Jesus contradictions that encompass our world, we need to question what our pastor or church tell us that we are supposed to believe about really any societal issue, and look at what the red-letter words of Jesus tell us. We need to look at the contrast between the White-Jesus ideology that is so pervasive in our culture and the red letters.

In the words of Jesus himself,

> "No good tree bears bad fruit, nor again does a bad tree bear good fruit; for each tree is known by its own fruit. Figs are not gathered from thorns, nor are grapes picked from a bramble bush. The good person out of the good treasure of the heart produces good, and the evil person out of evil treasure produces evil; for it is out of the abundance of the heart that the mouth speaks."
>
> Luke 6:43–45

When we evaluate how White-Jesus Christians treat people and the result is exclusion, hurt, condemnation, and damnation, they cannot be seen as a "good" tree. When we look at people groups like the LGBTQ+ community, which are nonjudgmental, loving, kind, and generous, they look a hell of a lot more like a "good" tree. You see, the ways of the red letters do not produce hurt. On any issue, regardless of circumstance, we can always filter our beliefs in actions through the ways of the red letters. Beliefs that are formed on a foundation of true, generous, bold love.

Chapter 15
BE THE CHANGE

Blessed are those who are humble in a world of egocentrism, for theirs is the kingdom of God.

Blessed are those who are hurting and those who hurt for the hurting, for they will be comforted.

Blessed are those who truly listen instead of eagerly waiting to talk, for they will inherit the earth.

Blessed are those who hunger and thirst for change, for they will be filled.

Blessed are those who feel compassion, for they will receive compassion.

Blessed are those who keep it real, for they will see God.

Blessed are the peacemakers who stand in the tension, for they will be called children of God.

Blessed are those who have been hurt by the wrath of religion for trying to follow the ways of Jesus, for theirs is the kingdom of heaven.

Blessed are you when the religious folk hate on you and try to falsely roast you because of your red-letter ways. Brush it off—hell, celebrate it—for your reward is great.

* * *

Our world has been a mess for a hot minute, and we are done with our procrastinating ways. Today is the day to do something about it; today we start a revolution based on red-letter love.

And when I say a revolution, I mean a change-the-poorly-written-history-books kind of revolution. And when I say we, I am talking about you reading these words right now, and I'm not speaking hypothetically.

History is filled with world-changing movements, both bad and good. For a movement to be successful (which this one will be because it's clear we have had enough), there has to be unity and solidarity among the people. All who are interested in seeing a red-letter revolution: we need to find one another, and we need to do our best to *be the change* daily, in grand or subtle ways. Don't discount your ability to change the world, because we need you, right now, in this moment. You can't sit by and do nothing at all and hope it changes on its own. It won't. We need to see a unification based on humility, empathy, compassion, and standing boldly for love in the midst of tension.

I know in this huge world, it's easy to feel small when we talk about big change. It's easy to feel as if we are not qualified, not smart enough, not rich enough, not educated enough, not old enough, not young enough, not established enough to ourselves be the change we think the world needs.

My friend, the belief that you cannot make a difference is the most tragic lie we could ever allow to go unchecked. It's the lie the people of Germany told themselves before it was too late. It's the lie we tell ourselves our whole lives that holds us back from truly great things. It's this lie that will try everything it can to hold us back from loving boldly.

Can I tell you my favorite story about Jesus?

A Pharisee asked Jesus if he wanted to come hang out
and eat at his house. So Jesus went to the Pharisee's house
and took his place at the dinner table.

And a woman in the city, who was a sinner, having learned that [Jesus] was eating in the Pharisee's
house, brought an alabaster jar of ointment. She
stood behind him at his feet, weeping, and began to
bathe his feet with her tears and to dry them with her
hair. Then she continued kissing his feet and anoint-
ing them with the ointment. Now when the Pharisee who had invited him saw it, he said to himself,
"If this man were a prophet, he would have known
who and what kind of woman this is who is touching
him—that she is a sinner."

Jesus spoke up and said to him, "Simon, I have
something to say to you."

"Teacher," he replied, "speak."

"A certain creditor had two debtors; one owed
five hundred denarii, and the other fifty. When they
could not pay, he canceled the debts for both of them.
Now which of them will love him more?"

Simon answered, "I suppose the one for whom he
canceled the greater debt."

And Jesus said to him, "You have judged rightly."

Then turning toward the woman, he said to
Simon, "Do you see this woman? I entered your
house; you gave me no water for my feet, but she has
bathed my feet with her tears and dried them with
her hair. You gave me no kiss, but from the time I
came in she has not stopped kissing my feet. You did
not anoint my head with oil, but she has anointed my
feet with ointment. Therefore, I tell you, her sins,

which were many, have been forgiven; hence she has shown great love. But the one to whom little is forgiven, loves little."

Luke 7:37–47

Do you know what Jesus is saying here?

He's not just saying, "Hey Simon, stop being such a jerk to this woman."

This lady had a serious past. Yet the world around her was changing. There was this guy who had ignited the most influential revolution based on love. Do you think she felt qualified to be part of that movement? Or do you think maybe she was so overwhelmed by it all that she broke down, crashed a dinner party, bawling and rubbing fancy oil on a guy who was changing her world. Maybe she felt her past and even her present disqualified her from being part of the change.

But what did Jesus make clear was the reality? He said that those who have been forgiven much, love much. And those who have been forgiven little, love little.

And I don't think he was implying that she just had so many more sins than the Pharisees and needed more forgiveness. What I feel like he was saying is that those who humbly acknowledge that they are screwed-up people (which we all are) are those who are real enough to accept forgiveness.

I don't know about your life but, especially in my younger days, I was a mess, and when I got into social justice, I often felt as if I was not good enough, that I was inadequate, to make real change. When I first started trying to follow the ways of Jesus, I knew that because of my lovely mess of a life I would never be able to have an impact as strong as those straight-edged hipster Christians. The belief that I wasn't good enough shut me down and held me back for years. And the thing is—it was all bullshit.

Jesus is straight up saying that those of us who are a mess are those who love most boldly. If anything, our struggles that we may feel some shame about make us more qualified to step up and join the resistance.

Y'all, Jesus was never the goody-goody, white, Christian boy that our grandparents told us he was. Jesus was the risk-taking, boundary-breaking smartass your grandparents warned you about, because he hung out with the wrong crowd. So if you think you have too much on your record to run with Jesus, I hope you know that you are more than good enough and that you are needed in this revolution of love. I hope you know that you truly are a bold truth seeker, lover, and warrior in this resistance. I hope you let the red letters of the radical, refugee Messiah guide you, not your white Jesus.

Epilogue

A LOVE STORY

It was November of 2016 and I was sitting on our cozy sunporch on a bright, sunny Iowa day. The sky had been gray for what felt like an eternity, and the sunshine brought warm comfort to my struggling soul.

My husband, Rich, was sitting across the room in his insanely comfortable faux leather chair that the cat has scratched to shit, reading something that must have been super interesting on his phone. I'm not sure what.

Really, I wasn't paying too much attention to what he was doing because I was too busy staring out the window, stuck within my own thoughts on life, liberty, and the pursuit of happiness. I was trying to figure out how our nation—in particular, much of the American Church—got to this point. The immediate grief and depression from the night of the presidential election was over, and now I was left confused and angry. Why did they empower a man who is the definition of a hateful bigot to lead our nation? How can someone claim this guy was chosen by Jesus to bring greatness to America? Why do people actually think Jesus even cares about American greatness? How does any of what is going on line up with the red letters?

I forced myself to leave the comfy porch chair that had become a soothing place and safe place to calm my anxiety in that moment, ran into the living room, grabbed my laptop, and started typing.

At this point in my life, writing was something I loved, but it was just a hobby. With the persuasion of my husband, I had started a blog called *Purple Hyacinths* about seven months prior, but I didn't post a ton of content. I was far too afraid to expose my soul to the world.

When I began writing that November day on my porch, it was one of those wildly fulfilling moments when the words that were completely unplanned came as natural as breathing.

After typing a couple pages, I looked at my husband, who was still just chillin' on his phone, and announced rather impulsively, "I think I am supposed to write a book someday. I mean, maybe. But if I do, I'm going to call it *Not Your White Jesus*."

"Cool, I think you should do it. What's it going to be about?" My husband responded in his usual encouraging manner that makes the seemingly impossible feel totally possible.

"I don't know. I guess Jesus. Like the real-life Jesus, not the Republican, Make America Great Again, white Jesus. You know, the Palestinian refugee guy who was all about love."

"Well, I think you should. What can I do to help?" asked Rich.

"I don't know." I said. "It's really just a thought."

And that was the truth: I didn't know. I just wrote some words down and felt like someday, when I was much older and wiser and not terrified of vulnerability—maybe I would write a book. And I left it at that.

* * *

As the calendar turned to 2017, I came to the general conclusion that I didn't know what the hell I was actually doing
with my life. I had taken the leap to quit teaching and start
working alongside Rich with The Nations while subbing
part-time, but I was still trying to find my place in the world.

I had just turned thirty; shouldn't I have it all figured
out by now?

Like much of the world, I was also full of tension and,
honestly, I was angry with the hate and vibrant contradic-
tion between much of American Christianity and the ways
of their Savior. I couldn't fathom how someone who had
even read a few of the red letters could use their fabricated
version of White Jesus to rationalize the egocentric oppression of others.

It was overwhelming.

So with Rich's encouragement, I decided that I
needed to take the month of January off from subbing and
basically spend time writing and soul-searching or something along those lines. My expectation was that if I took
this month off, I would have some great epiphany. My life
and purpose would become clear with a laid-out path I
could simply follow into my destiny.

But apparently that's not really how life works. After
about three weeks I had come to no grand conclusions
about my purpose, and I felt even more inner frustration
with the world in addition to the financial stress of taking
time off for what felt like a complete waste of time. Maybe
I had made a dumb decision; I mean, money was already
tight.

A few days before the end of January, I was sitting at
a coffee shop, probably pouting about my poor decision-
making skills and how much the world sucked, and I
thought back to the few pages I had written on that sunny

day in November. Without really thinking, I pulled up that writing that I hadn't looked at for two months and effortlessly turned it into a blog post and put it up on my little blog. Then I did something really out of character: I started sharing this writing publically. Like with the world. Yeah, I felt super uncomfortable, but hell, I couldn't think of a good enough reason not to.

The thing was, to my incredible shock, people actually started reading my writing. People related and shared my frustration with the hurt we were seeing caused by this White-Jesus ideology that runs rampant in our nation. There was a unity forming between people all over the world who longed to see the real red letters of Jesus win.

So I decided to change my blog title to *NotYour WhiteJesus.org* and started writing regularly. Within weeks, I began to share my writing on *Patheos* and the *HuffPost* and became a regular contributor to both sites. It felt surreal. More than that, through this newfound community of love seekers, I found incredible hope in a messy world of overwhelming hate.

* * *

And here we are in 2018. This morning I burnt the crap out of my left index finger and thumb on my hair straightener, and I am currently sitting in a coffee shop with my fingers taped up with burn gel and an ice pack. I literally have no chill. But like the throbbing pain we saw throughout 2017, the burn won't be the end of it.

In 2017 we saw hate rise to a new level in our nation. It was the year that illuminated the oppression and corruption we face every day in this "free" nation. It was the year that followers of White-Jesus thought they had won.

But 2017 is also the year when we began to find a deeper unity in the common desire to love. The year that sparked a red-letter revolution. The year when I learned no matter my insecurities, I was born to be part of this resistance, and you are too. Because of 2017, we will no longer buy into the lie that we can't change the world. We know that together the world will change because of love.

My friend, the world will change because you are love. We are love. And together love always wins. Twenty-seventeen was not a tragedy; it was the hard start of a beautiful love story.

ACKNOWLEDGMENTS

To my badass husband, Richard, thank you for being my constant and unwavering encouragement, feeding me amazing food on the regular, and taking care of everything for everybody all of the time so that I could pursue this dream that you always believed in, even before I did. You are my favorite human, and I am so grateful that you are my person. I love you to Andoria and back!

To my beautiful daughter Hayley, you are the coolest and bravest truth-seeking love warrior I know. You are the most amazing and compassionate kid ever, and I am proud and thankful beyond words that fifteen years ago, someone decided I should be your mom. I love you infinitely, and I can't wait to watch your journey continue to unfold. I have no doubt that you are going to change the world.

To my amazing son Hendrix, you bring more joy into the lives of everyone around you than anyone I have ever encountered. You are an adventurous and loving spirit, and I am so grateful to get to be your mom. I love you a million.

To my bonus daughter Laila, you are the funniest and most creative human I know. You have an amazingly compassionate soul. I love your face, and I cannot wait to see what life has in store for you.

To my bonus son Ethan, you have such a kind spirit, and your eye for catching the beauty all around you in pictures is incredible. I am so grateful to have someone to help me figure out design. I love you, and I know that you will be an amazing architect/photographer/interior decorator.

To my best friend in the universe, Dawnie, no words will ever be adequate to express how grateful I am for your soul. I wouldn't have made it through life without you. You are the most beautiful and giving person I know. You are the loving spirit our world needs desperately. I love you indefinitely.

To my Dad, thank you for always believing in me regardless of if you agree with my views, and thank you for showing me unconditional love, especially through the teenage years. I love you very much.

To Papa and Bina, thank you for the structure and love y'all gave me during a time in life when I needed it the most. I will always be thankful; I love y'all very much.

To my Mom, thanks for always offering refuge when life is turbulent. Love you tons.

To Bill, thank you for being an awesome person and a real, Jesus-following pastor. I am so grateful for all the conversations and coffees we have shared over the past twenty years. Love you.

To Betsy, thank you for your amazing, kind, and constantly giving heart. I am very thankful and lucky to have you in my life. Love you.

To Wendy, thank you for being one of my heroes and inspirations. You have such a beautiful and unique soul, and you are going to be the best doctor in the history of ever. Love you, sister.

To Kate, thank you for how hard you fight for what you believe in. Love you also, littlest sister.

To Chris, thank you for your constant kind spirit; you are an awesome human. Love you, bro.

To Nyan, Anya, and Grayson, I love you guys. Y'all are the future, and I am incredibly grateful to be related to all of y'all.

To Jessica Miller Kelley, thank you for messaging me on Facebook and believing that now is the time to resist and let love win. I am incredibly grateful to have been able to work with you.

To everyone at WJK, thank you for your desire to see love win and for believing in the idea behind this book. I am endlessly grateful.

To the O.G. readers of *NotYourWhiteJesus.org*, y'all are a constant reminder that no matter how messy our world may feel, because of people like you, there is always hope.

To all of y'all truth seeking love warriors, thank you for boldly being the change that our hurting world needs. You are the ones who will change the world. You are amazing humans who will let love win. Don't ever forget you are everything we need.

DISCUSSION GUIDE

Chapter 1: Not Your White Jesus

1. What has been your experience with white American Christianity? What social or political views do you associate with Christianity in America today?
2. What role has religion played in your life? Has it been a source of life, hurt, or both? Talk about your experiences.
3. Read Matthew 1:18–2:23. How do you think the early experiences of Jesus and his family affected the man he would become? What has been your experience with the ways of the Jesus of the red letters?

Chapter 2: Meet the Brown-Skinned, Palestinian, Red-Letter Jesus

1. If you close your eyes and picture the real-life, historical figure of Jesus—the guy that used to hang on the shores of a big ole lake grilling fish with his buddies—what does he look like? Why do you think he looks the way he does in your mind?
2. Have you experienced the culture of the Middle East or had contact with people from that region? When have

you learned something important from someone who looked different from you?

3. Read Matthew 5, 6, and 7. What major themes do you notice in Jesus' famous Sermon on the Mount?

Chapter 3: Hey, Neighbor

1. Why do we tend to fear people who are different from us? Do you think it's possible to love people while simultaneously fearing them?

2. In the story of the Good Samaritan (Luke 10:25–37), why do you think Jesus made the "enemy" the hero? What examples can you think of in the news today of people you wouldn't expect doing good things?

3. Read Luke 6:27–36. Have you ever experienced a perceived enemy's kindness toward you? If so, what impact did it have on you?

Chapter 4: Selling Tickets to Heaven

1. Why do you think so much of white American Christianity focuses more on the Great Commission and what may happen after we die, than the Great Commandment to love God and neighbor? Have you ever felt the pressure to convert others to Christianity? If so, discuss your experience.

2. Read Matthew 23:13–15. How does Jesus' warning about conversion efforts line up with his call to "make disciples"? How does it line up with the Great Commandment?

3. Do you talk about your faith with others? Why or why not? What are your motivations or concerns about doing so?

Chapter 5: More Humble Than You Would Think

1. How would you describe people in your life who show great humility? Is there a connection between self-esteem and humility?
2. Read Luke 14:7–14. How could you apply these red letters to your own life? In what situations are you tempted to "take the best seat"?
3. Have you ever thought of humility as an action? What actions could you practice to embrace the red-letter way of humility?

Chapter 6: Bleeding Hearts and Bold Love

1. Can you think of a time when you avoided seeing others in pain? How did you avoid it and why?
2. When was the last time you cried for the hurting? Did "suffering with" others lead you to take any particular action?
3. Read Luke 19:41–46. How were empathy and anger linked for Jesus?

Chapter 7: Speak Loudly: Silence Is Complicity

1. Has there ever been a situation in which you saw oppression and stayed silent? Do you think speaking up would have changed anything? When have you spoken up against injustice?
2. Read Matthew 23. Why do you think Jesus so broadly and publicly called out the Pharisees? Does the harshness of his words challenge your impression of Jesus?
3. Many activists say that "silence is violence." What do you think that means? How does staying silent affect

those being oppressed? How does staying silent affect you?

Chapter 8: Can We Stand in the Middle?

1. In following Jesus, do you believe it is possible to love boldly while taking the middle ground? Why or why not? Why do you think Jesus did things that were against cultural norms and made people uncomfortable?
2. Read Luke 12:49–53. What do these shocking red letters tell you about the bold positions Jesus wants us to take?
3. In a nation where racism runs rabid, what actions can you take to help enable love to win?

Chapter 9: Unexceptional Exceptionalism

1. Do you think God wants America to be great? What would this mean? Does God care more about the well-being of people based on their nationality?
2. Read Luke 4:14–30. Why do you think Jesus' allusions to serving non-Jews upset people so much? Why didn't Jesus come to Make Israel Great Again?
3. How do you think Jesus would deal with the American nationalism of White-Jesus Christianity today?

Chapter 10: Ban the Walls

1. White-Jesus Christianity often says it is not "smart" to let refugees or immigrants into the U.S., worrying about jobs, resources, and terrorism. How do you think these concerns align with the red letters?

2. Read Matthew 25:31–45. Who do you see as sheep and goats in America today? How can we treat refugees and immigrants today the way we would treat Jesus himself?

3. When exclusion is the law of the land, how can we personally become more inclusive?

Chapter 11: Making War, Not Peace

1. Why do you think Jesus never "stood his ground" when people wanted to kill him? What can we learn from this on both a personal and national level?

2. What do you think Jesus would say to the NRA and pro-war White-Jesus Christianity if he was here today?

3. Read Matthew 5:38–45. Do you think it is wise (or even possible) to live out the radical nonviolence Jesus talks about?

Chapter 12: Living the Dream

1. In what ways do you struggle with consumerism? What changes might you need to make?

2. Read Luke 12:13–21. How do you see people "building bigger barns" today? Is Jesus telling us not to plan for the future?

3. How does Jesus' statement, "You cannot serve God and wealth" (Matt. 6:24) make you feel?

Chapter 13: Not Here for Your Enjoyment

1. How has the church or the wider culture affected your perspective on sex, dress, or gender norms? What has been positive? What has been negative?

2. Read Mark 14:3–9. What dynamics do you notice between Jesus, the woman with the ointment, and the other men at the table? What can we learn from Jesus here?

3. Why do you think White-Jesus Christianity struggles with treating women with respect as equals, when we see Jesus valued women so greatly?

Chapter 14: Squad Goals

1. Have you ever seen or experienced prejudice from the American Church? Have you ever been complicit in perpetuating such prejudice? Have you even stood up against it?

2. Read Matthew 9:9–13. Why was the religious establishment so appalled by the people Jesus hung with?

3. What are some ways we can reach beyond our usual social circles to connect with people different from us— especially those marginalized by the church and society?

Chapter 15: Be the Change

1. What do you think Jesus meant when he said, "Those who find their life will lose it, and those who lose their life for my sake will find it" (Matt. 10:39)?

2. What small, subtle things can you do to practice red-letter love? What bigger things can you do?

3. Read John 14:8–15. Have you ever felt like you're not good enough to have an impact on the world? How do Jesus' words inspire you to boldly make change in our world today?

NOTES

Chapter 1: Not Your White Jesus

1. "Child Poverty," *National Center for Children in Poverty*, http://www.nccp.org/topics/childpoverty.html.

Chapter 3: Hey, Neighbor

1. Gregory A. Smith, "Most white evangelicals approve of Trump travel prohibition and express concerns about extremism," *Fact Tank*, Pew Research Center, February 27, 2017, http://www.pewresearch.org/fact-tank/2017/02/27/most-white -evangelicals-approve-of-trump-travel-prohibition-and-express -concerns-about-extremism/.

Chapter 4: Selling Tickets to Heaven

1. "Reigning with Christ: The Original (And Still Greater) Great Commission," *Do the Word*, November 19, 2012, http:// dotheword.org/2012/11/19/reigning-with-christ-the-original -and-still-greater-great-commission/.

Chapter 8: Can We Stand in the Middle?

1. Martin Luther King Jr., "Letter from Birmingham City Jail," April 16, 1963, Teaching American History, http:// teachingamericanhistory.org/library/document/letter-from -birmingham-city-jail/.

Chapter 10: Ban the Walls

1. "ICE ERO Immigration Arrests Climb Nearly 40 Percent," ICE, updated November 2, 2017, https://www.ice.gov /features/100-days.

Chapter 11: Making War, Not Peace

1. "A Report to the National Security Council—NSC 68," Truman Papers, April 12, 1950, https://www.truman library.org/whistlestop/study_collections/coldwar/documents /pdf/10-1.pdf.

2. Niall McCarthy, "The Top 15 Countries for Military Expenditure in 2016," *Forbes*, April 24, 2017, https://www.forbes .com/sites/niallmccarthy/2017/04/24/the-top-15-countries-for -military-expenditure-in-2016-infographic/#e1a66ed43f32.

3. "Global Peace Index 2017, " Vision of Humanity, http:// visionofhumanity.org/indexes/global-peace-index/.

4. Belinda Goldsmith, "Just 10 Percent of World Military Spending Could Knock Off Poverty: Think Tank," *Reuters*, April 4, 2016, https://www.reuters.com/article/us-global -military-goals/just-10-percent-of-world-military-spending -could-knock-off-poverty-think-tank-idUSKCN0X12EQ.

Chapter 13: Not Here for Your Enjoyment

1. Penn Bullock, "Transcript: Donald Trump's Taped Comments about Women," *New York Times*, October 8, 2016, https://www.nytimes.com/2016/10/08/us/donald-trump-tape -transcript.html.

Chapter 14: Squad Goals

1. "Nashville Statement," The Council on Biblical Manhood and Womanhood, 2017, https://cbmw.org/nashville-statement.